Especially For

....

From

....

Date

....

Women

of the
BIBLE

Devotional

Inspiration from the Lives, Loves, and
Legacy of Notable Bible Women

Women
of the
BIBLE
Devotional

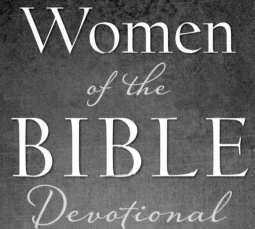

Inspiration from the Lives, Loves, and
Legacy of Notable Bible Women

BARBOUR BOOKS
An Imprint of Barbour Publishing, Inc.

Welcome to the

WOMEN *of the* BIBLE *Devotional*

--- ···❧·❧··· ---

The women of the Bible are a colorful group
of people. Some, like Mary, our Lord's mother, give us a
wonderful picture of faith. Others, like Jezebel or Delilah,
are strong warnings against sin. Then there are the
seemingly ordinary women, perhaps those who get one
small mention in scripture, whose lives seem much like
our own.

Every woman in the Bible has a story, whether short
or long, and through each, God shows us some truth in
His Word. Sometimes these women help us understand
an important spiritual truth, or they illustrate a problem
we've faced in our own barely functional or clearly faith-
filled lives. But no matter the success level of a biblical
woman's life—or our own—on truth remains secure: God
shows His enduring love through every believer's life.

God loves women—those who lived thousands of years ago and those who live today—and the examples of both can shine through with the ultimate truth of His love. The women described here lead us through the rough-and-tumble elements of this world to the peace that comes from knowing Him.

As a bonus to the stories of these biblical women, this volume includes alphabetical lists of the meanings of some women's names that appear in the Bible. These appear on pages 19, 30, 41, 52, 63, 74, 85, 96, 107, 118, 129, 140, 151, 162, 173, 184, and 193.

DAUGHTERS OF PHILIP: *Encouragement*

---

*Leaving the next day, we reached Caesarea and stayed
at the house of Philip the evangelist, one of the Seven.
He had four unmarried daughters who prophesied.*
ACTS 21:8–9 NIV

On the way to Jerusalem, Paul stopped at Caesarea to stay with Philip the evangelist, one of seven men who, along with Stephen, had been chosen to care for the Hellenistic Jews who had been overlooked in church food distributions (Acts 6:1–5). When Paul visited, four daughters lived in Philip's household, all of whom were believers and who prophesied.

How proud Philip must have been of his household full of girls. In so many homes the faithful are mixed with those who lack faith or who are at best lukewarm, but Philip's lifework outside the home had also impacted his own family, and the truths he shared were being passed on through his children. It *was* a legacy to be proud of, one that testified both to his own consistency of faith and action and God's work in his family's lives. God gave Philip an important role, to nurture these four gifts whom God had given him.

Do you have a family member who is faithful to God? Pass on your pride in her willingness to serve Him. Encourage her on days when life is being difficult. And let her know that she is loved every day, even on the hard ones!

THE VIRTUOUS WOMAN: *A Blessed Attitude*

—— ···✦·✦··· ——

Charm is deceptive, and beauty is fleeting;
but a woman who fears the LORD is to be praised.
PROVERBS 31:30 NIV

A lot has been written about the Proverbs 31 woman. It's easy to think that there wasn't anything this woman couldn't do. It's probably not an exaggeration to suggest that most of us feel intimidated by her. We feel insignificant next to this woman who did so much.

But break this proverb down and you'll see that there isn't much difference between the Proverbs 31 woman and us. Yes, the time, place, and culture weren't the same, but there are plenty of other similarities between her and us. This woman did the same things we do. She took care of her family, looked for bargains, extended a helping hand, honored her husband, loved her children, met the needs of others, planned, shopped, and trusted God. We do those things.

So where might the difference between her and us be noticeable? How about attitude? The Proverbs 31 woman fully relied on God as she went about her day. She lived out this Bible verse: "Whatever you do, work at it with all your heart, as working for the Lord, not for human masters" (Colossians 3:23 NIV).

The Proverbs 31 woman sets an example for us of what happens when we love the Lord and desire to serve Him. Let's not be jealous of her, let's learn from her. We'll be blessed if we do.

JEMIMAH, KEZIAH, AND KEREN-HAPPUCH:
Job's Daughters

—— ···❖❖❖··· ——

*And he also had. . .three daughters. The first daughter he named Jemimah,
the second Keziah and the third Keren-Happuch. . .and their father
granted them an inheritance along with their brothers.*
JOB 42:13–15 NIV

Job's daughters were given to him as part of a restoration package.
Job lost family, wealth, and health. Devastated, he came face-to-face with
God, where spiritual revelations changed Job's perspective and character.
Afterward, God restored his children, wealth, and health.

The daughters God gave Job, Jemimah, Keziah, and Keren-Happuch,
were known as the most beautiful women in the land. They were also
atypical in another way: Job gave them an inheritance. Job's daughters
received vast wealth, which can also symbolize a spiritual inheritance.

We can share in the spiritual inheritance passed to these daughters.
One of the facets of that inheritance is insight into suffering.

Job's daughters must have learned firsthand from their dad that we
never suffer alone. Many centuries before the birth of Christ, Job declared,
"I know that my redeemer lives, and that in the end he will stand on the
earth" (Job 19:25 NIV). When we suffer, we have Christ's company.

Job also declared that while we may never know the why of suffering,
we can trust the God who allows it. His wisdom is higher than ours. As Job
said, "My ears had heard of you but now my eyes have seen you. Therefore I
despise myself and repent in dust and ashes" (Job 42:5–6 NIV).

When you suffer, remember that you share in the spiritual legacy of
Job's daughters today.

KEZIAH: *God Knew Her Name*

••• ❦ ••• ❦ •••

He named. . . the second [daughter] Keziah.
JOB 42:14 NIV

Keziah is the second daughter of Job, born after Job's great suffering and restoration. It is noteworthy that her name and the names of her sisters are recorded in scripture, while her brothers are not named.

We do not know why Keziah and her sisters are the ones mentioned, but we do know that God knows His people by name and that He calls a person by name to declare that that person has been selected for a divine task.

That God knows you by name reveals the personal and familiar nature of the relationship He's counting on building with you. Isaiah 43:1 (NIV) says, "I have summoned you by name; you are mine." As someone who is known by and belongs to God, you can be confident of His protection, His company, and His belief in your potential.

God says He calls us by name because He wants us to know him (Isaiah 45:4). Knowing God is an endeavor we are all called to and one more than worthy of our life's energies.

Sometimes, God calls us by name to reveal a specific task He desires us to perform. When we sense God calling our names, let's strive to be like Samuel, who answered God's voice by saying, "Speak, LORD, for your servant is listening" (1 Samuel 3:9 NIV).

ELIZABETH: *Nothing Is Impossible with God*

——— ••• ✦ ◦ ✦ ••• ———

"What's more, your relative Elizabeth has become pregnant in her
old age! People used to say she was barren, but she has conceived a son
and is now in her sixth month. For the word of God will never fail."
LUKE 1:36–37 NLT

When an unexpected impossibility becomes reality, a miracle materializes. Elizabeth dreamed of having a child. She waited most of her life, and finally the news of her pregnancy became true. Her miracle not only fed her faith but also encouraged the mother of Jesus.

Mary must have been overwhelmed by all the news: to be a virgin and find out she was pregnant and the child she was carrying was the Son of God was a huge shock. Then she learned her cousin, Elizabeth, was also pregnant. The angel used Elizabeth's amazing news to reassure Mary that her extraordinary experience came from God.

It is hard to discern truth at times. We hear vague comments like, "Your difficulty will someday pass," or, "Eventually you will see the lesson in a loss."

What helps most in times of confusion is to touch something real and authentic. Mary knew Elizabeth. They both were pregnant. And at Elizabeth's older age, Mary knew this could only be a gift from God. The news of Elizabeth's pregnancy gave Mary hope and comfort as she entered an unknown future.

God is very economical—He often acts in ways that not only bless one person but many. As His grace showers on one, He provides for others. One blessing multiplies into many miracles. Nothing is impossible with God.

RAHAB: *Outliving the Past*

— ••• ❖•❖ ••• —

In the same way, was not even Rahab the prostitute considered
righteous for what she did when she gave lodging to the spies
and sent them off in a different direction?
JAMES 2:25 NIV

Two women are named in the Faith Hall of Fame found in
Hebrews: Sarah, Abraham's wife, and Rahab. Later, in the New Testament,
James again holds Rahab as an example of faith.

When the spies Joshua sent to Jericho sought refuge at the prostitute's
hostel, they couldn't have guessed her lasting legacy. She never outlived her
past. The epistles breathe "Rahab the prostitute" in a single breath, similar
to "Ivan the Terrible" or "Mean Joe Green."

Rahab's former occupation made her the ideal example of true faith.
A Canaanite idol worshipper was bad enough. A prostitute who might
have worked at a pagan temple in no way deserved a place in the line of the
Messiah. But as we read in Ruth 4 and in Matthew 1, David was Rahab's
great-great-grandson. Through him, the Messiah came.

If God could use a prostitute to bring a Savior to the world, what will
He do with us? Sometimes, God gives us new names with our new birth.
Jacob the deceiver became Israel the prince. Other times, He asks us to
wear our label proudly.

We may have a label we wish we could drop, a past we want to erase.
But maybe God wants to flaunt that weakness to showcase His grace.

MARY OF BETHANY: *Cut to the Chase*

―――― ⋯ ⟡ ⟡ ⋯ ――――

When Mary reached the place where Jesus was and saw him, she fell at his
feet and said, "Lord, if you had been here, my brother would not have died."
JOHN 11:32 NIV

When Jesus visited Mary and her siblings, Martha and
Lazarus, Mary dropped everything to listen to His teaching—something
far more important than gourmet meals or dust-free furniture. Mary loved
Jesus, and He loved her and her family.

When Lazarus became seriously ill, the sisters sent Jesus a message,
confident He would come immediately and heal him.

But Jesus did not come. Lazarus worsened and died.

When the Healer finally approached Bethany, Martha left to meet
Him. Mary, however, remained at home until Martha returned and said,
"Jesus is asking for you."

Mary hurried to see Him and fell at His feet. This time, though, no
starry-eyed gaze met His. Tears poured down Mary's cheeks. She blamed
His delay for Lazarus's death. Where had Jesus been when Mary needed
Him most?

Women did not reproach a rabbi in that manner. Jesus could
have turned His back on Mary. But her honesty did not damage their
relationship. Jesus cried with Mary. Then He gave her the surprise of her
life: Lazarus, alive again.

Like Mary, we can be honest with Jesus when we do not understand
what He is doing in our lives. He will not turn away. And He has a plan
that's bigger and better than we can imagine.

THE WEALTHY WOMAN OF SHUNEM:
Generous Heart

--- ••• ❧•❧ ••• ---

One day Elisha went to the town of Shunem. A wealthy woman lived there,
and she urged him to come to her home for a meal. After that, whenever he
passed that way, he would stop there for something to eat.
2 KINGS 4:8 NLT

It was a simple trip through town, one that Elisha had taken
before. This time, however a Shunammite woman extended an invitation
to Elisha to share a meal with her family. Her hospitality didn't stop there;
she prepared a room in her house and invited Elisha to stay there when
he was in town.

The Shunammite woman saw a need. Added to that awareness was
her willingness to take what she had and use it to meet that need. It meant
giving of her time, energy, and money.

When Elisha asked her if there was anything he could do to repay her
for her kindness, she told him no. She was quite content with what she
had. Eventually she was blessed with a son, but this was not a blessing she
had sought after.

Let's pray and ask God for an attitude like the Shunammite woman's.
Let's ask God to keep our eyes open to how we might minister to others.
Let's also ask God to keep us from falling into the trap of thinking that little
acts of service aren't important. It's often these small gestures of kindness
that reach the furthest.

THE LOOSE WOMAN: *Steer Clear*

--- ··· ❦ ❦ ··· ---

Wisdom will save you from the immoral woman,
from the seductive words of the promiscuous woman.
PROVERBS 2:16 NLT

The loose woman mentioned in Proverbs is a prostitute, a woman who provides sexual activity for a price. Proverbs describes her as loud, defiant, brazen, undisciplined, and ignorant. She provides favors to the highest bidder. Self-indulgence is at the heart of her activity.

In the book of Proverbs, men are advised to steer clear of loose women, and the Bible clearly declares that the prostitute and those who keep company with her are on the way to death. The prostitute's activity of self-indulgence is judged as detestable—displeasing to God and worthy of complete and utter punishment.

However, in the Old Testament stories about prostitutes, God also includes the promise that He will forgive and establish loving, healthy relationships with loose women if they repent and turn to Him. In the Gospels, Jesus acts out this truth by seeking out, forgiving, and healing prostitutes.

This is a poignant reminder that no matter what our sin, God is always ready to forgive and restore so that we can enjoy a relationship with Him. "You will remember your sins and cover your mouth in silent shame when I forgive you of all that you have done. I, the Sovereign LORD, have spoken!" (Ezekiel 16:63 NLT).

ABIGAIL: *Too Risky?*

--- ••• ❖•❖ ••• ---

One of Nabal's servants went to Abigail and told her, "David sent messengers
from the wilderness to greet our master, but he screamed insults at them.
These men have been very good to us, and we never suffered any harm from them.
Nothing was stolen from us the whole time they were with us. In fact,
day and night they were like a wall of protection to us and the sheep."
1 SAMUEL 25:14–16 NLT

Nabal, a wealthy man, must have been a serious risk taker.
David had asked for food for his soldiers, who had protected Nabal's
flocks and shepherds from David's battles with Saul and had never
plundered so much as a lamb. Yet this greedy man who owned three
thousand sheep turned the dispossessed but mighty warrior down. Did
Nabal even begin to understand the danger of having warriors with
sharp swords on his front doorstep?

Though Nabal didn't recognize the riskiness of his greed, his servant
did and ran to Nabal's wife, Abigail. A few words made her recognize the
danger, not only from David, but possibly from God, since David was His
anointed king, and his Lord might take up the justice of his cause. Abigail
understood those risks and didn't want to take them. She immediately
brought David the food, and her quick action barely saved the lives of her
entire household.

Like Abigail, we, too, often face spiritual risks associated with greed.
Can we recognize them and avoid being destroyed by our possessions?

What Did That Woman's Name Mean?

Just as today, some biblical names had meanings. Here are a few of those meanings, including names of some women in this book.

Abi: Fatherly

Abiah: Worshipper of God

Abigail: Source of joy

Abihail: Possessor of might

Abijah: Worshipper of God

Abishag: Blundering

Abital: Fresh

Adah: Ornament

MERAB: *Who Wants to Be a Princess?*

--- ••• ❧•❧ ••• ---

Surely the lowborn are but a breath, the highborn are but a lie.
If weighed on a balance, they are nothing.
PSALM 62:9 NIV

Merab, King Saul's elder daughter, reveled in the best
of everything: exquisite food, beautiful clothes, lavish entertainment. She
expected nothing less throughout her lifetime, for as Merab matured,
aristocratic men wanted to marry her.

Saul offered his daughter's hand to whoever defeated Goliath, the
Philistine giant. Jealous when David succeeded, Saul then promised Merab
to David if he continued to conquer Israel's enemies. The shepherd turned
soldier appeared reluctant because of his humble background, so Merab
was married to Adriel of Meholah (1 Samuel 18:18–19).

However, David married her sister Michal. How did Merab react?
Perhaps, for the first time, she had not received the deference she expected.

Her royal blood later proved deadly to her descendants. During
Saul's reign, he apparently massacred the Gibeonites, whom Israel had
promised to protect. They demanded David surrender seven of Saul's male
descendants to make amends. Five of the men David handed over to be
executed were Merab's sons (2 Samuel 21:8–9).

Our own lifestyles may seem at best, boring, and at worst, drudgery.
But as Merab's story demonstrates, wealth and pedigree do not always
deliver happiness. They may even prove disastrous to our families.

Whether rich or poor, though, we can become children of the King.
Through His Son, Jesus, we can possess ultimate security and heavenly
treasure.

What more could a princess want?

JOANNA AND SUSANNA: *A Life of Freedom*

••• ❦•❦ •••

*Joanna, the wife of Chuza, Herod's business manager; Susanna;
and many others who were contributing from their
own resources to support Jesus and his disciples.*
LUKE 8:3 NLT

Joanna and Susanna were two of many women who joined
Jesus' band of followers. In Jewish culture, women were not permitted
to associate with rabbis, and by keeping company with Jesus and by
supporting his followers (many of them men) with their own resources,
these women stepped out of cultural roles.

Maybe they opted out of cultural roles because of gratitude. Jesus had
saved them from disease or met their great need, compelling them to leave life
as they'd known it to devote themselves to service and generosity. Or maybe
the freedom from bondage to disease or evil spirits that Jesus had provided
buoyed them and prompted them to seek freedom in every area of life.

Wherever Jesus goes, He promises freedom. "I will free your
prisoners. . . . Never again will an oppressor overrun my people"
(Zechariah 9:11, 8 NIV).

In what areas of life do you long for freedom? Maybe you yearn to be
free from disease, destructive habits, debilitating emotions, or others'
expectations. Ask Jesus for freedom. He came to set you free in every area
of life, just as He set Joanna and Susanna free.

Pursue Jesus until He pries your bonds loose. Then respond with
authentic gratitude and a life of service.

WIDOW OF NAIN: *Grief and Healing*

Soon afterward, Jesus went to a town called Nain, and his disciples and a large crowd went along with him. As he approached the town gate, a dead person was being carried out—the only son of his mother, and she was a widow.

LUKE 7:11–12 NIV

Becoming a widow is life changing. During this time in history the agony a widow experienced was added to by the culture. A woman counted on her husband for her security. If he died, a woman was dependent on her son for help. If her son perished, the widow was truly at a loss.

This is what the widow of Nain faced. Bereft of a husband and now burying her son, one can only imagine the fear, anxieties, and questions running through her mind. How was she going to survive? What would become of her now? However, in the midst of her son's funeral, Jesus appears. Moved with compassion, Jesus restores the woman's son to her.

When we face a loss, Jesus is there. God gives us these words of assurance: "The LORD is close to the brokenhearted and saves those who are crushed in spirit" (Psalm 34:18 NIV).

We'll experience grief in our lives. We'll also experience healing. The widow's grief was healed immediately. For us the healing process takes place over time. We can be certain it will happen, though, because Jesus' compassion never ends. As He reached out to this widow, He also reaches out to us.

EUODIA AND SYNTYCHE: *Fighting among Friends*

— ••• ❖❖ ••• —

Now I appeal to Euodia and Syntyche. Please, because you belong to the
Lord, settle your disagreement. And I ask you, my true partner, to help these
two women, for they worked hard with me in telling others the Good News.
They worked along with Clement and the rest of my co-workers,
whose names are written in the Book of Life.

PHILIPPIANS 4:2–3 NLT

Two teenage girls stood in the doorway, looking down at the
floor. Tension filled the air after harsh words had come between them.
One girl's mother intervened with the words, "You girls have a special
friendship. Don't let words come between you. What you have is rare.
Honor it. Preserve it. Friendship strengthens both of you."

Neither girl, now women, remembers the reason for the argument.
A mediator brought wisdom and calming perspective to the situation.
With the spirit of forgiveness, they let go and with love reestablished the
friendship that continues more than five decades later. They have seen
each other through challenging times of marriages, births, and deaths.
One brief moment could have unraveled the gift of a lifelong friendship
saved by wise words.

Paul saw the treasured gift of friendship between Euodia and Syntyche,
two hardworking, faithful women in Philippi. Settle your disagreement, he
counseled.

Arguments often destroy relationships. Words are spoken that would
be better left unsaid. Feelings get hurt, and it becomes difficult to forgive.

Differences in opinion can divide, but friendship is worth the effort.
With the salve of forgiveness, a dose of love, and willing hearts to move on,
relationships can heal. Friendship is a treasure worth fighting for.

ABITAL: *Just a Footnote*

―――――― ⚜ ――――――

These are the sons who were born to David in Hebron. . . . The fifth
was Shephatiah, whose mother was Abital.
2 SAMUEL 3:2, 4 NLT

We can assume that Abital became David's wife or concubine
while he was still king of only Judah, since her son, Shephatiah, was born
in Hebron, where David ruled before Israel came under his command. But
unlike Abigail and Michal, we know nothing of this woman's relationship
with the king. Abital was one of David's lesser women and had none of the
stature of those honored wives whose stories are told along with his.

Not only is Abital simply a biblical footnote, so is her son, who
obviously never caused enough trouble to get him more than a brief biblical
mention nor did such outstanding good to receive a place in Jewish history.
Abital and Shephatiah may have been fine people, loved by friends and
family, but they didn't have a high position in the court, and Shephatiah was
a fifth son, with little or no stature.

But many ordinary, faithful people, who never stand out in a crowd,
are known and loved by God. Maybe, along with Abital and Shephatiah, we
are some of them. Though few people know our names or even our good
works, God does. And because we love and serve Him, even if it's quietly,
we'll also share eternity with Him.

RIZPAH: *Keeping a Vigil*

<hr />

Rizpah daughter of Aiah took sackcloth and spread it out for herself on a rock. From the beginning of the harvest till the rain poured down from the heavens on the bodies, she did not let the birds touch them by day or the wild animals by night.

2 SAMUEL 21:10 NIV

When the people of Israel first reached the Promised Land, they made an unwise but unbreakable vow with the Gibeonites. Centuries later, King Saul broke that vow, causing the death of many.

God brought a drought on Israel during David's reign because of Saul's misstep. Determined to make amends, David asked the Gibeonites how he could satisfy the wrong done against them. Their answer: let them kill seven of Saul's male descendants.

Without seeking God's will, David handed over Saul's descendants, including two sons of the royal concubine Rizpah. After torture, they were hung from trees and never buried.

Rizpah exchanged royal purple for rough burlap. She kept vigil as days turned into weeks, sleeping in snatches, chasing away carrion birds and scavenging animals. Nothing could shake her watchfulness.

Her bravery came to David's attention. He had the bodies cut down and buried in the family plot, along with the bones of Saul and Jonathan, which had been left unburied until that point. The drought ended.

Rizpah helped bring healing to a divided nation. Her act echoes the account of another brave woman. At the end of a difficult workday, Rosa Parks sat down on a bus.

Like Rizpah and Rosa, we can change the course of nations by one brave act.

MILCAH: *A Messianic Link?*

...·❧·...

I know that the LORD is great, that our Lord is greater than all gods.
The LORD does whatever pleases him, in the heavens and on the earth.
PSALM 135:5–6 NIV

Milcah, the wife of Abraham's brother Nahor, waved goodbye to her brother-in-law and his wife, Sarah. Milcah's relatives were moving from Haran, located in present-day Turkey, to Canaan (Genesis 12). She and Nahor remained prominent citizens of Haran, a busy commercial town dedicated to Sin, a moon deity. Perhaps their absorption of pagan culture prompted God's command that Abraham and Sarah separate themselves from family, a radical departure from the norm. Later scriptures demonstrate that Milcah's descendants reverenced both Yahweh (Genesis 24:50; 29:31–35) and idols (Genesis 31:29–30).

Milcah had little time to think about Abraham and Sarah, as she gave birth to eight sons (Genesis 22:20–23). Her days overflowed with diapering, refereeing, and nose wiping.

She probably did not ponder herself as a link in God's chain of events to redeem humankind. Yet, Milcah's son Bethuel fathered Rebekah and Laban. Their children, cousins Jacob and Leah, married and had Judah, whose tribe produced Jesus Christ.

Like Milcah, we permit busyness to blind us to God's plan and our place in it. We, too, absorb our culture and fail to worship Him.

Still, God uses our lives to accomplish His purposes, whether we welcome His sovereignty and grace or allow everyday pressures to smother His truth.

VASHTI: *The Put-Away Queen*

--- ···❖···❖··· ---

But when the attendants delivered the king's command, Queen Vashti
refused to come. Then the king became furious and burned with anger.
ESTHER 1:12 NIV

Queen Vashti was married to King Xerxes, a king prone to
impulsive behavior. King Xerxes was holding a banquet for his nobles and
officials along with other honored guests. After several days of feasting and
celebrating, he sent for Queen Vashti to come appear before him. The king
wanted to show his beautiful queen off to his party guests.

We don't know for sure why Queen Vashti said no to the king's
request. Perhaps she was agitated with King Xerxes and wanted to make
him look bad in front of his guests. Maybe it was humility that prompted
her response. She knew a lot of wine had been consumed, and she didn't
want to put herself in the position of being gawked at by people who had
had too much to drink. Whatever her reasons, her decision cost Vashti her
title as queen and the chance to ever come before King Xerxes again.

This is what decisions do. They come with blessings or consequences.
Perhaps that's why in the book of Haggai, God reminds us to "give careful
thought to your ways" (Haggai 1:7 NIV).

We'll face many choices in our daily living. And we'll face the results
of our decisions. Therefore, let's take the time to prayerfully seek God's
wisdom before deciding what we're going to do. We'll be glad we did.

JOCHEBED: *Creative Problem Solver*

--- ··· ❖ ❖ ❖ ··· ---

Amram and Jochebed became the parents of Aaron,
Moses, and their sister, Miriam.
NUMBERS 26:59 NLT

Jochebed had a trio of impressive descendants who were prominent in the rescue of the Hebrew people from Egypt. That the younger son, Moses, lived through infancy is remarkable, and his rescue may be attributed in part to his mother's ingenuity.

The Hebrew people were living as slaves in Egypt, and Pharaoh, feeling threatened by their increasing numbers, ordered that all Hebrew baby boys be drowned in the Nile. When the infant Moses grew too big to hide, Jochebed placed him in a papyrus basket and floated him on the Nile and into the arms of Pharaoh's daughter, who determined to raise Moses as her own.

This clever scheme thwarted the destruction Pharaoh had intended. Moses lived and eventually led God's people to freedom.

Sometimes life brings challenges that seem insurmountable. Imagine the terror Jochebed must have felt to birth a baby boy in the wake of Pharaoh's order that all baby boys be killed. Instead of allowing the perplexity of her circumstances to paralyze her, Jochebed implemented a creative solution.

When faced with perplexing challenges, ask God for creative solutions. He promises to provide help when we ask for it. "If you need wisdom, ask our generous God, and he will give it to you" (James 1:5 NLT).

THE ADULTEROUS WIFE: *A Narrow Place*

— ··· ⟡ ··· —

An adulterous woman is a deep pit, and a wayward wife is a narrow well.
Like a bandit she lies in wait and multiplies the unfaithful among men.
PROVERBS 23:27–28 NIV

Sexual temptation permeates our world, whether it's a
picture of a hunky guy or some handsome coworker standing before us. If
we're not careful to resist, the tentacles of desire quickly wrap around us.

Scripture makes it abundantly clear that unfaithfulness is no option
for the believer and gives us this picture of its dangers. God is not trying
to deny us some wonderful experience. He's warning that the lust that
appears so delightful leads us not to joy, but into a deep, narrow place that
destroys our lives.

Who would want to be a deep pit or a narrow well when she could
be so much more by following God faithfully and making life good for
many people? The godly woman described in Proverbs 31:10–31, who is the
opposite of the woman portrayed in this verse, has no narrowness about
her. Her life impacts others with good things, while this adulterous woman
is busy kidnapping innocent (or not-so-innocent) men and drawing them
into her own narrow place.

God gives every woman a choice: faithfulness and a broad life or a
narrow life bound up in sexuality. Though the physical attractions of a
moment may have short-term appeal, in the long run, no narrow well
allows anyone to live with joy.

What Did That Woman's Name Mean?

Just as today, some biblical names had meanings. Here are a few of those meanings, including names of some women in this book.

Ahinoam: Brother of pleasantness

Ahlai: Wishful

Aholibamah: Tent of the height

Aksah: Anklet

Anah: Answer

Anna: Favored

Atarah: Crown

Eve: *The Blame Game*

———— ··· ❧ · ❧ ··· ————

The man replied, "It was the woman you gave me who gave me the fruit,
and I ate it." Then the LORD God asked the woman, "What have you done?"
"The serpent deceived me," she replied. "That's why I ate it."
GENESIS 3:12–13 NLT

Adam blamed Eve. Eve blamed the serpent. Each pointed
the finger of responsibility elsewhere. Though both of them knew the rules
and both failed to follow God's guidelines, they never confessed their own
participation in their disobedience to God.

After all these years, we, too, continue to play the blame game. We
attribute all our difficulties on the government, society, and even our
families. "If only this hadn't happened" or "I just couldn't help it" justifies
our behavior. We even blame restaurants for our obesity. Blaming becomes
our excuse for bad decisions, actions, and lack of action.

God knew Adam and Eve had eaten from the tree of the knowledge of
good and evil. He still came to them, asking them what happened, offering
a chance to confess their disobedience. They chose to avoid the truth.

God knows when we fail to follow Him, when our hearts stray.
He comes to us, asking us to talk with Him, to tell Him about our
transgressions. We know there will be consequences to any misbehavior,
and it is hard to admit we were wrong.

God doesn't want our excuses; He wants us. We need to quit playing
the blame game, one we can never win. God stands ready to forgive and
receive us with love as winners with Him.

Rahab: *Waiting and Watching*

She said to them, "Go to the hills so the pursuers will not find you. Hide yourselves there three days until they return, and then go on your way."
Joshua 2:16 NIV

Before Jericho's walls fell down, before the Israelites even crossed the Jordan River, Joshua sent two spies to Jericho.

They set up shop with Rahab, who conspired against the king of Jericho to allow them to escape safely. Then she hung a red cord on the wall, expecting protection during the upcoming battle. She couldn't have guessed how long the wait would be.

Let's pretend January is the first month of the Jewish calendar (it's not, of course). But Rahab's year started something like this:

January 1–3: Spies arrive and escape with her help.

January 10: The Israelites cross the Jordan River (Joshua 4:19).

January 14: The weeklong Passover celebration begins (Joshua 5:10).

January 22: After the weeklong Passover, the Israelites march around Jericho for six days.

January 28: The Israelites march around Jericho seven times and the wall falls down, with the exception of Rahab's home—four weeks since their arrival.

Like Rahab, we are often caught "in between." We have dropped our red cord of faith. When we ask God, "When?" He says, "Soon." The problem is, God's definition of "soon" doesn't agree with ours.

Never doubt God is at work during that in-between time. Let Him prepare you—and others—for what lies ahead.

THE APOSTLES' WIVES: *Part of the Ministry*

--- ⋯ ✦ ⋯ ---

*Don't we have the right to food and drink? Don't we have the right
to take a believing wife along with us, as do the other apostles
and the Lord's brothers and Cephas?*
1 CORINTHIANS 9:4–5 NIV

Paul had a problem to address. Issues were being raised about a
wife traveling with her husband, and a double standard was developing. So
Paul took exception to this and spoke out about it.

Life as an apostle was not easy. In fact, it was a lot of work. There
was travel involved and politics to put up with. Enemies arose and the
environment could be hostile. Apostles were often at the mercy of others to
provide them with food, shelter, or work. They faced times of harassment,
torture, and sorrow.

How comforting it must have been to the apostles to have their wives
traveling with them. Their wives' encouragement would have made a big
difference in their ministry. Knowing someone "had their backs" probably
helped them react with more boldness and confidence.

The wife who traveled with her husband was also being blessed. She
had the opportunity to impart her knowledge of Christ to other wives and
women. She shared in the rejoicing when someone accepted Christ. She
heard the Gospel repeatedly, which strengthened her own faith.

These wives' prayers, service, and encouragement had an impact on
those who took God's word into the world. They set an example. Let's do
our best to follow it, whether or not we're married.

MIRIAM: *Bossy Big Sister*

— ••• ❦ ••• —

If you harbor bitter envy and selfish ambition in your hearts,
do not boast about it or deny the truth. Such "wisdom" does not come
down from heaven but is earthly, unspiritual, demonic.
JAMES 3:14–15 NIV

"*Moses shouldn't have taken a* Cushite wife," Miriam
muttered to Aaron. "As Israel's leader, he shouldn't have married a foreign
woman. But our little brother thinks he knows everything."

"You're a prophetess, too," Aaron agreed, "and I'm the high priest.
Moses might occasionally ask *our* opinions."

Before long, God summoned the three siblings to the meeting tent.
He spoke from a pillar of cloud to Miriam and Aaron. "My servant Moses. . .
is faithful in all my house. With him I speak face to face. . . . Why then were
you not afraid to speak against my servant Moses?" (Numbers 12:7–8 NIV).

When the cloud lifted, Miriam screamed, "Leprosy! I'm a leper!"

Aaron begged his brother to forgive their sin and help their sister.

Moses cried, "Please, God, heal her!"

He did, but commanded Miriam be banished outside the camp for
seven days.

During that miserable week, she must have struggled. Why did
God punish her, when Aaron, too, was involved? The scriptures say
Aaron instantly repented, whereas we see no evidence Miriam regretted
her rebellion. Perhaps bossy big sister required time to rethink her
relationship with God and with her family.

Sometimes we need to do the same.

KETURAH: *In the First Wife's Shadow*

— ••• ❧❧❧ ••• —

Then again Abraham took a wife, and her name was Keturah.
GENESIS 25:1 KJV

Keturah became Abraham's wife sometime after his first wife Sarah's death. Married to the aged Abraham, Keturah undoubtedly compared her life with that of Abraham's first wife, Sarah. She had heard of Sarah's unparalleled beauty (it was legendary in those times), and she knew that Sarah's son Isaac would always have more status than her sons. However, Keturah bore Abraham six sons. Most likely she lived a life of wealth, prestige (she was married to a great man), and fulfillment (in those days a wife's greatest role was to bear sons to carry on her husband's name).

We don't know if Keturah felt as if she lived in Sarah's shadow or if knowing she enjoyed less prestige than her husband's first wife irked her as it might us.

When we live in someone's shadow, we can remember that the Bible advises us not to compare ourselves with those around us but to faithfully perform the duty that God has assigned to us. Second Corinthians 10:12–13 (NIV) says, "We do not dare to classify or compare ourselves with some who commend themselves. . . . We. . .will not boast beyond proper limits, but will confine our boasting to the sphere of service God himself has assigned to us."

We can concentrate on the sphere of duty God has assigned us and count on Him to bless us.

GOMER: *Straying from God's Faithfulness*

—— ···✦··· ——

Then the LORD said to me, "Go and love your wife again, even though she commits adultery with another lover. This will illustrate that the LORD still loves Israel, even though the people have turned to other gods and love to worship them."

HOSEA 3:1 NLT

Unfaithful Gomer left her husband, Hosea. Abandoning their children, she turned to the temptations of the world and evil desires. Eventually she found herself in slavery, imprisoned by her sins.

God instructed Hosea to find Gomer and bring her home. Hosea was to keep her safe and provide for her. Most important, Hosea was to love her once again.

Gomer represents the people of Israel. God tells this story to show His willingness to find them, to protect and provide for His nation. He rescues His people from their sins and brings them back to His heart filled with unconditional love.

But Gomer symbolizes us, too, because we stray from God's commands. The lure of temptations seduces us away from God's ways.

Always God is faithful. He finds us where we hide in the dens of lust and greed. He brings us home to His heart. In His forgiving nature, God constantly seeks to restore our relationship with Him. He stands firm in His commitment to love us unconditionally.

God's unfailing love heals our souls and serves as a model on how we are to treat others.

Like Gomer, we are unfaithful. But God's faithfulness is forever.

AKSAH: *Boldly Ask*

―――――― •••• ⤜⬦⬦⤛ •••• ――――――

One day when [Aksah] came to Othniel, she urged him to ask her father for a field. When she got off her donkey, Caleb asked her, "What can I do for you?" She replied, "Do me a special favor. Since you have given me land in the Negev, give me also springs of water." So Caleb gave her the upper and lower springs.
JOSHUA 15:18–19 NIV

Othniel, Aksah's cousin, took the city of Keriah Sepher to win her hand, as her father Caleb had demanded. But once they were wed, Aksah realized they had a problem: though they had land, which her father had given them as her dowry, the property lacked the water that would make crops grow. So she returned to her father and asked him for more property that held springs. Graciously, though by law Caleb didn't have to, he agreed to provide for the newlyweds. Obviously this hero of Israel loved his daughter deeply.

In his generosity to his daughter, Caleb paints a picture of our heavenly Father. Though He has given us so much, we still have daily needs. Do we come to Him boldly, knowing that, like Aksah's father, He will not fail us? Unlike Othniel, who may have hesitated to ask his father-in-law for too much, do we come with confidence in His love for us, though the request may seem large? Or will doubts keep us from enjoying the springs that could fill our lives with joy?

RHODA: *Are You Crazy?*

—— ···◆◆◆··· ——

When she recognized Peter's voice, she was so overjoyed she ran back without opening it and exclaimed, "Peter is at the door!" "You're out of your mind," they told her.
ACTS 12:14–15 NIV

The apostle Peter had been captured. The church expected him to follow in the footsteps of James, who had been martyred only a short time earlier.

Mary, the mother of John Mark, opened her home for a prayer meeting. Perhaps their prayers echoed their earlier prayer to "enable your servants to speak your word with great boldness" (Acts 4:29 NIV). They didn't expect deliverance.

Mary's household servant Rhoda remained on duty. In spite of their dangerous situation, they trusted her with the important job of answering the door. She let believers slip in and out as required. They must have trusted her common sense and ability to think on her feet.

No one expected Peter to show his face. When he arrived, Rhoda was so flabbergasted that she left him on the street while she ran to tell the others.

She interrupted the prayer meeting with her good news. Instead of shouting hallelujah, they called her crazy.

Today people may call us crazy for believing in a dead Messiah. They might say we're deluded to trust an unscientific book.

Like Rhoda, we can boldly proclaim the good news in spite of a disbelieving response.

A TREASURED WIFE: *A Gift from God*

The man who finds a wife finds a treasure,
and he receives favor from the Lord.
PROVERBS 18:22 NLT

The word treasure brings many images to mind: gold coins, silver pieces, gemstones, and other precious jewels. It makes us think of a treasure chest hidden away. Perhaps we're reminded of a tale of adventure in which "X marks the spot." Sometimes treasures are those items languishing in an attic, whose value is only realized years later.

What is it that makes a wife worthy of being called a treasure? Perhaps it's due to her qualities. She is a partner, a companion, a helpmate. She is trustworthy, reliable, and a friend. The biggest reason, however, that a wife is considered a treasure to behold is because this is how God considers her.

When God created Eve, He remarked, "It is not good for the man to be alone. I will make a helper suitable for him" (Genesis 2:18 NIV). The wife's role is designed by God. From early times we see that she fulfills a position in a man's life that no one else does.

Not every woman ends up being a wife. Instead of being discouraged, remember that friendliness, trustworthiness, and helpfulness aren't attributes assigned to wives alone. We should all strive to make these qualities a part of our daily lives.

If we do, we'll have a treasure worth sharing.

JEZEBEL: *A Bold Woman*

--- ❖ ---

Jezebel his wife said, "Is this how you act as king over Israel? Get up and eat!
Cheer up. I'll get you the vineyard of Naboth the Jezreelite."
1 KINGS 21:7 NIV

Jezebel, a king's wife remembered for treachery and brutality, knew what she wanted and boldly pursued it. Once, she schemed to acquire a vineyard for her husband. She had the vineyard's owner falsely accused and consequently stoned, leaving the vineyard for her husband to snatch.

Nothing stopped her bold pursuit of her evil ambitions. In this life, she got what she wanted. And she encouraged her husband to pursue his selfish wants, no matter whom the pursuit harmed.

Our culture admires the traits Jezebel exercised to extremes. She was bold. She made things happen. She motivated others to make things happen. However, Jezebel lacked a moral compass. When she set on a course of action, she acted without considering whether it was morally right or wrong.

She displayed supersized selfishness.

We can admire her traits, like boldness and drive, but not her motives. When selfishness propels success, we must change our course.

Boldness prompted by love for Christ plays out very differently from boldness prompted by love of ourselves.

When we act boldly we must make sure our acts are prompted by Christ's love, and we can know that Christ's love will infuse us with boldness. "Therefore, since we have such a hope, we are very bold" (2 Corinthians 3:12 NIV).

What Did That Woman's Name Mean?

Just as today, some biblical names had meanings. Here are a few of those meanings, including names of some women in this book.

Athaliah: God has constrained

Azubah: Desertion

Baara: Brutish

Bashemath: Fragrance

Bathsheba: Daughter of an oath

Bathshua: Daughter of wealth

Bernice: Victorious

GREEK WIDOWS: *Taking Care of All*

---- ❖ ----

*But as the believers rapidly multiplied, there were rumblings of discontent.
The Greek-speaking believers complained about the Hebrew-speaking
believers, saying that their widows were being discriminated against
in the daily distribution of food.*

ACTS 6:1 NLT

Taking care of the widows was an early church policy. Special
consideration was given to those who lacked economic means, legal
position, and protection in that society. Those with more assets helped the
widows, especially with the basics of food and shelter.

But one segment of this group appeared to be neglected. The Greek
widows came from a different culture and background. They probably
spoke a strange language and may even have looked different. Their care
was overlooked and forgotten.

Perhaps the inattention to the Greek widows came from the rapid
growth of believers. When things expand quickly, mistakes can be
made. We don't know for sure if the treatment of the Greek widows was
accidental or intentional discrimination. But believers began to notice a
distinction was occurring between the groups, with one being treated
better than another.

God's generosity comes without judgment. He doesn't see us in classes
with labels or whether we are accepted or not. The color of a believer's
skin or the origin of her family roots makes no difference to Him. He cares
for every individual as she is, and we are to model Him in this attitude, too.

God's love is all encompassing, and His care embraces everyone. He
loves and takes care of all.

The Woman Who Saved a City: *Speak Up!*

--- ❦ ❦ ---

While they were battering the wall to bring it down, a wise woman called from the city, "Listen! Listen! Tell Joab to come here so I can speak to him."
2 Samuel 20:15–16 niv

Joab and his men were in pursuit of Sheba, a man who had rebelled against David. Sheba was hiding out in the city, and Joab planned on tearing the walls town, literally, in order to get him.

As the battering began to pound on the city walls, a woman of the city asked to speak to Joab. She told him about the people inside and their faith. Joab said his only interest was Sheba. Once he got him, Joab would leave them in peace. The woman said they'd take care of Sheba, and the town was saved.

What did it take for this woman to speak up? Courage? Yes, but what else? Did she have to push away the naysayers who said she was wasting her time, because Joab wouldn't listen to her? How much fear did she swallow in order to go stand on the front lines? Did she worry about convincing the city's inhabitants of her plan?

Speaking up can be scary. Too often we fall into the mind-set of believing that our one voice won't make a difference. Yet there is account after account in the Bible of how one person's faith, spoken out loud, changed lives. God can do amazing things with your faith-filled words.

So speak up!

NAOMI: *Matchmaker Extraordinaire*

Oh, the depth of the riches of the wisdom and knowledge of God!
How unsearchable his judgments, and his paths beyond tracing out!
ROMANS 11:33 NIV

Because of her daughter-in-law Ruth's loving care, Naomi's depression in losing her family lifted. The barley Ruth gleaned from Bethlehem's surrounding fields eased Naomi's fear of starvation. One day, Ruth brought home food the fields' owner had urged upon her.

When Naomi learned Ruth had gleaned in Boaz's fields, her eyes brightened. "That man is our close relative; he is one of our guardian-redeemers" (Ruth 2:20 NIV). Her mental wheels began to turn as Boaz showed increasing interest in Ruth. He potentially could secure Ruth's future and her own. Naomi instructed her daughter-in-law to take the initiative. But she knew better than to treat the situation as a business negotiation.

"Wear your prettiest dress," Naomi urged Ruth. "Use your nicest perfume when you go to the threshing floor to see Boaz."

When the captivated man arranged to marry Ruth, Naomi no doubt congratulated herself on her excellent matchmaking skills. The stability both she and Ruth craved was sealed by the couple's wedding. A son born to them filled Naomi with joy—a grandson, at last! Her friends praised God as she cared for little Obed.

As Naomi cuddled him, she had no idea God had used her matchmaking to accomplish a bigger purpose. Obed later had a son named Jesse, the father of King David—the ancestor of God's Son, Jesus Christ.

What is God doing in our lives as we follow Him faithfully?

RACHEL: *Transformation*

—— ···⟡·⟡··· ——

*As she [Rachel] breathed her last—for she was dying—she named her son
Ben-Oni. But his father named him Benjamin. So Rachel died and was
buried on the way to Ephrath (that is, Bethlehem).*
GENESIS 35:18–19 NIV

Say "Bethlehem," and people worldwide think of King David's
birthplace as well as the town where Mary gave birth to our Savior. It
attracts more than two million visitors every year.

No such happiness awaited Rachel in Bethlehem. The birth of Joseph
had lifted the stigma of "barren" from her. Years later, she spent her second
pregnancy on the road from Haran to Canaan. Her pains came on when
they reached Bethlehem. After a prolonged and difficult delivery, Rachel
knew her end was near. She named her boy "the son of my sorrow." But his
grieving father renamed him "the son of my right hand," Benjamin.

Centuries later, King Herod slaughtered the infants of Bethlehem.
Matthew pointed to Rachel's pain when he quoted from Jeremiah. "A
voice is heard in Ramah, weeping and great mourning, Rachel weeping
for her children and refusing to be comforted, because they are no more"
(Matthew 2:18 NIV). For the mothers of Bethlehem, their cries deafened
them to the birth of the Messiah.

Often God works like that. Death and life walk side by side. He
transforms our place of suffering into a place of new life, hope, and joy.
Let's offer our grief to God for transformation.

NAAMAN'S WIFE'S MAID: *Acting in Faith*

---

*And she said unto her mistress, Would God my lord were with the prophet
that is in Samaria! for he would recover him of his leprosy.*
2 KINGS 5:3 KJV

The maid who served Naaman's wife was a young Israelite girl
who had been captured, taken to a foreign country, and forced to serve in
Naaman's household.

We would understand if this young trauma survivor felt despair. We
would understand if she felt bitterness directed at God and Naaman, the
valiant commander who had contributed to the military victory over the
maid's country.

However, when she learned that Naaman was afflicted with leprosy,
she acted with faith and love. She told her mistress of the prophet in
Samaria, who directed Naaman to a cure.

May we follow her example and express faith and love in difficult
circumstances. Faith is the key to overcoming so many challenges. As Jesus
said, "Truly I tell you, if you have faith as small as a mustard seed, you can
say to this mountain, 'Move from here to there,' and it will move. Nothing
will be impossible for you" (Matthew 17:20–21 NIV).

The maid's faith expressed in love is worth noting and emulating. Her
life was an example like the one described in 2 Corinthians 2:14 (NIV): "But
thanks be to God, who always leads us as captives in Christ's triumphal
procession and uses us to spread the aroma of the knowledge of him
everywhere."

ANNA: *A Shared Message*

···❧···

And there was one Anna, a prophetess. . .which departed not from the
temple, but served God with fastings and prayers night and day. And she
coming in that instant gave thanks likewise unto the Lord, and spake of
him to all them that looked for redemption in Jerusalem.
LUKE 2:36–38 KJV

When Jesus and His parents first came to the temple,
Simeon quickly recognized the baby Messiah. Then he didn't hesitate to
share that good news with someone he knew would appreciate it: Anna,
a prophetess who spent all her time in the temple, making God the focus
of her existence. You've heard of people who seem to live at church? Well,
Anna literally lived at the temple, fasting and praying night and day.

Delighted at the message that God's salvation had come, Anna
believed, knew the news was not for her alone, and began to share it with
other Jews who knew the scriptures and had also been looking for God's
promised Savior.

Just as Anna's joy welled up from the news Simeon shared, something
wells up in our lives, too. Are our lips bubbling with good news or gossip?
With encouragement or bitterness? We're going to share something with
our world—something based on the central core of our lives. Will it be the
joy of the Lord or something else? What's the focus of that message that we,
even unintentionally, share?

WOMAN WITHOUT DISCRETION: *Poor Choices*

—— ••• ❧•❧ ••• ——

*Like a gold ring in a pig's snout is a beautiful woman
who shows no discretion.*
PROVERBS 11:22 NIV

The Bible paints a very unsettling picture of a woman who doesn't know how to exercise good judgment. Being compared to a pig, even one beautified by a gold ring in its snout, is not something women strive for. However, this image paints a perfect picture of indiscretion.

Why is being discreet so challenging? Could it be because discretion takes discipline? Choosing to be sensitive to others, not engaging in gossip, restraining ourselves from indulgence, and exercising modesty take commitment. When we don't make conscious efforts at discernment, we find ourselves heading off in a direction that doesn't honor God.

Being discreet has some wonderful blessings. According to Proverbs, "Discretion will protect you, and understanding will guard you" (Proverbs 2:11 NIV). Think of all we're protected from if we practice discretion. We won't be apologizing for unkind speech or dealing with the effects of overindulgence. People can take us at our word and count on us to keep their secrets and not gossip.

Every day we face choices. The food we eat, the places we go, the way we spend our time and money, the words we say, the way we serve, our responses to God are all choices.

Therefore, let's exercise discretion. Let it be said of us, as it was for the woman in Proverbs 31, that we speak with wisdom and have faithful instruction on our tongues.

HAGAR: *The God Who Sees Me*

••• ◦❧◦❧◦ •••

Thereafter, Hagar used another name to refer to the LORD,
who had spoken to her. She said, "You are the God who sees me."
GENESIS 16:13 NLT

Invisible to the elite, Hagar was used, abused, and
considered a piece of property. After all, she was just a slave, a nobody,
and seen as having little value. Who would ever notice her absence? Who
would miss her when she was gone?

But God watched over Hagar. He knew what was happening in her
life and noted the details of her circumstances. He came to help, guide,
and provide for her and showed this struggling woman that she, too, was a
child of God, valued, accepted, and loved.

At times in our own lives, we may feel we don't matter. We can't see
that our lives are making any difference. Maybe our actions go unnoticed;
our attempts to reach out are unseen. We feel alone and of little worth.

Just as God watched over Hagar, He guards us, too. Because He calls
us His children, we know we are His loved ones whom He valued enough
to redeem with the high price of His Son's life. Not only has He saved us,
no matter who else ignores us, He has rescued us from invisibility.

Let's begin our prayer today with the words "You are the God who
sees me" and embrace the One who creates our worth, defends our souls,
and loves us without end.

NOAH'S WIFE: *Her Home Was a Zoo*

··· ❖ ···

The LORD then said to Noah, "Go into the ark, you and your whole family,
because I have found you righteous in this generation."
GENESIS 7:1 NIV

"God told you what?" Noah's wife knew her husband's
revelation about filling an enormous boat with animals would only confirm
their neighbors' conviction that Noah had lost his mind.

His wife knew better. Noah loved God, and that love spilled over into
his relationships with her, their sons and daughters-in-law, and even their
neighbors. If anyone heard from God in these corrupt days, it would be
Noah.

As he built the ark, she sometimes found God's plan hard to believe,
especially as their friends' derision hardened into hostility. But she
supported him. When animals miraculously arrived, two by two, she
shared Noah's joy that God had confirmed His Word.

The elation probably dwindled when Noah's wife became a zookeeper.
Distributing food and shoveling tons of manure felt less than spiritual. How
she must have missed her home and grieved for family and friends who had
rebelled against God. What would the future hold? Would she ever gain
her land legs again?

Living through storms and unglamorous circumstances, we may share
the doubts and weariness Noah's wife felt. But like her, we have witnessed
God's faithfulness. He prepared Noah's wife for a new life she could not
have imagined, and He will do the same for us.

RUTH: *A Stranger Among Us*

——— ··· ❖·❖ ··· ———

Ruth fell at his feet and thanked him warmly. "What have I done to deserve
such kindness?" she asked. "I am only a foreigner."... "May the LORD,
the God of Israel, under whose wings you have come to take refuge,
reward you fully for what you have done."
RUTH 2:10, 12 NLT

The people of Bethlehem liked to pigeonhole people: Naomi
the bitter, Ruth the foreigner—Rahab the prostitute, who became Ruth's
mother-in-law.

Boaz's parents aren't mentioned in the genealogy connecting Boaz
and Ruth to King David at the end of the book. At some point, Ruth must
have learned the miraculous story of how God saved Rahab when Jericho
was destroyed. The family that had once welcomed a former prostitute
wouldn't hesitate about a woman who had claimed her mother-in-law's
faith as her own.

It couldn't have been easy. More than most, Boaz knew both the
challenges and blessings of marrying outside the twelve tribes. Even so,
he chose Ruth, unafraid of whatever difficulties they might face. Her faith
and her beauty spoke on her behalf. Even so, Ruth could hardly believe she
had found his favor. Through them, God would bring the Messiah into the
world.

As surely as God brought Ruth in contact with the one man who could
best accept her past, He will direct our paths to people who understand
us. Together, we grow stronger and in turn reach out to others. Only God
knows how far our lives will reach.

What Did That Woman's Name Mean?

Just as today, some biblical names had meanings. Here are a few of those meanings, including names of some women in this book.

Bithiah: Daughter of God

Chloe: Green

Cozbi: False

Damaris: Gentle

Deborah: Bee

Delilah: Languishing

Dorcas: Gazelle

MARTHA: *Choosing Faith*

···❖···

Jesus told her, "I am the resurrection and the life.... Do you believe this, Martha?"
JOHN 11:25–26 NLT

Martha's brother Lazarus lay dying, and she sent for Jesus. Martha counted on Jesus to heal Lazarus. But Jesus arrived too late to help—it seemed. By the time he arrived in Bethany, Lazarus had been entombed four days.

When Martha learned that Jesus was nearby, she left the guests—who, according to custom, had come to her home to comfort her—and went to meet Jesus. The Bible doesn't say so, but perhaps this act indicated that Martha, who had once implored Jesus to chastise Mary for not working diligently to host their guests, had learned to look beyond caring for the guests' physical needs to focusing on faith. Or perhaps Lazarus's death prompted Martha to prioritize faith and eternal matters.

When she reached Jesus, He offered her an opportunity to speak her faith. Despite her sorrow and possible disappointment that Jesus had arrived too late, Martha declared her faith. " 'Yes, Lord,' she told him. 'I have always believed you are the Messiah, the Son of God, the one who has come into the world from God' " (John 11:27 NLT). A few hours later, Jesus granted new life to the deceased Lazarus. Lazarus walked out of the tomb!

Life offers many opportunities in which we can choose between doubt and faith. When faced with that choice, despite suffering, despite feeling let down by God, we can choose faith. God will come through.

THE DESTITUTE WIDOW: *An Abundance of Oil*

—— ···◆◆◆··· ——

*Elisha replied to her, "How can I help you? Tell me,
what do you have in your house?" "Your servant has nothing there at all,"
she said, "except a small jar of olive oil."*
2 KINGS 4:2 NIV

A widow had a problem. A debt had been amassed. With her husband dead and no way to pay, her children were going to be taken from her as payment. She appealed to Elisha to prevent this from happening. His solution was for her to gather up as many jars as she could, take what oil she had, and pour it into the jars.

The widow did as instructed and was amazed that jar after jar filled with oil. When there were no more jars left, Elisha instructed her to sell the oil and pay off her debt. Whatever was left over would be enough to support her and her sons.

How the widow handled her problem says a lot about her. She was courageous to seek out Elisha. At the same time she was humble. She admitted to having a problem she needed help with and was willing to work to solve her problem. It would have been a difficult task to gather up the jars, fill them, and then go sell them.

Boldness, humbleness, and a willingness to work should be the attitudes we pray for when we face a problem. This approach worked for the widow, and it will work for us.

HANNAH: *Praying and Praising with Joy*

------------- ··· ❧ ··· -------------

*"My heart rejoices in the LORD! The LORD has made me strong. Now I have
an answer for my enemies; I rejoice because you rescued me. No one is holy
like the LORD! There is no one besides you; there is no Rock like our God."*
1 SAMUEL 2:1–2 NLT

Hannah's heartbreak over her childlessness unfolded
into praise and rejoicing. And not once in her prayer thanking the Lord for
giving her a son did she claim any credit, brag about her faith and sacrifices,
or attempt to bargain for more blessings. She gave God all the credit.

Hannah could have simply thanked God for answering her plea.
But after expressing her gratitude, she turned her focus on God as He is,
acknowledging Him as the source of her strength. She affirmed God as the
sovereign King and held fast to God, clinging to His promise. Her words
show great faith.

We might expect that Hannah's song would have been all about her
appreciation of God for giving her a son. But most of her hymn praises God
for His faithfulness and goodness.

Like Hannah, we can also make our prayers center on God. Answered
prayers fill us with wonder and gratitude. Thankfulness ignites our praises,
and we turn our attention to the God of the universe whose strength and
faithfulness constantly surround us.

Proclamations of His attributes and praises for His name can also
overflow in our prayers. Then, like Hannah, we'll be remembering it isn't
about us; it's all about God.

ASENATH: *God's Bounty*

—— ••• ❧ ••• ——

Before the years of famine came, two sons were born to Joseph
by Asenath daughter of Potiphera, priest of On. Joseph named his firstborn
Manasseh and said, "It is because God has made me forget all
my trouble and all my father's household."
GENESIS 41:50–51 NIV

After Joseph explained Pharaoh's dream to him and the
delighted ruler made him second in command of his land, Pharaoh gave
him another blessing: a wife from a priestly family. We don't know what
kind of theological challenges this created in their marriage, but it seems
Asenath made Joseph happy, if this description of his first son's naming is
anything to go by.

In an age when most families had many children, it's a bit surprising
that Joseph and Asenath had only two. But two were enough for God's
purpose—in a time when infant and child mortality was high, both boys
grew and thrived and became joys to their father (Genesis 41:51–52; 50:23).

Why were there no more children? Perhaps Asenath had secondary
infertility, or maybe she died—scripture never tells us. But whatever the
story is behind this wife of the man who virtually ruled Egypt, we know
that God did provide—perhaps not as generously as we might have
expected, but fully all the same. Two sons filled the need of Joseph and
Israel, as God had planned.

When we, too, don't receive overflowing bounty, can we trust that
God has given enough? Or will we demand more of something we don't
quite need?

MARY, MOTHER OF JESUS: *Blew It?*

---

*"For whoever does the will of my Father in heaven is my brother
and sister and mother."*
MATTHEW 12:50 NIV

Mary and Jesus' brothers had traveled from Nazareth to the shores of the Sea of Galilee—a long, weary walk—to see Him. Yet upon their arrival, Jesus said, "Who is my mother, and who are my brothers?" (Matthew 12:48 NIV).

That reception raised their eyebrows! But Mark's Gospel (3:21) tells us Jesus' family did not visit merely because they missed Him. His outrageous claims that He could forgive sins and that He was Lord of the Sabbath had stirred up trouble with the Pharisees. His brothers and mother feared Jesus was "out of his mind" and had decided to take charge of Him.

The scriptures do not tell us exactly what went through Mary's mind during this difficult time, but her memories of Gabriel's visitation, Jesus' miraculous birth, God's intervention with Joseph, and the worship of shepherds and wise men seemed to have faded.

With this question, Jesus confronted Mary's possible lapse of faith. He stretched His hands toward His followers, recognizing them as His spiritual family who did God's will by believing in His Son.

The Bible does not describe Mary's immediate reaction. But one thing is clear: she and Jesus' brothers did not take Him back to Nazareth and curtail His ministry.

Will we, too, follow God's will, instead of following only our own logic?

THE WOMAN OF SAMARIA: *Tough Outside*

············· ❧ ·············

Many of the Samaritans from that town believed in him because of the woman's testimony, "He told me everything I ever did."
JOHN 4:39 NIV

She had perfected her tough shell. Each pain, each bad decision, added layer after layer until no one paid attention anymore.

Each husband left more quickly than the one before. Her current lover hadn't even bothered with marriage. Why pretend? She kept to herself.

Going to the well at noon allowed her to avoid the finger-pointing women. The presence of a man surprised her—a *Jewish* man. She decided to ignore him.

Instead, He stopped her. "Will you give Me a drink?"

Maybe He wanted what most men did. She flirted with Him. "You are a Jew. . . . How can You ask me for a drink?"

His answer piqued her interest, when He said of Himself, "He would have given you living water." Then He pinpointed her unsavory history and debated religious questions.

Most amazing of all, He revealed His identity to her. She returned to town and ran through the streets, shouting the news. "The Messiah is here!"

Jesus cracked her cocoon with a few compassionate, honest questions and answers.

Life has given most of us calluses of some form or other. But Jesus waits to bathe us in the living water, to remove our thick, tough cover and allow our hearts to grow soft and fresh.

ZEBUDAH: *Have an Impact*

--- ···◆·◆··· ---

Jehoiakim was twenty and five years old when he began to reign;
and he reigned eleven years in Jerusalem. And his mother's name
was Zebudah, the daughter of Pedaiah of Rumah.
2 KINGS 23:36 KJV

Zebudah had some interesting family connections. Her father, Pedaiah, was part of the group that helped repair the city walls of Jerusalem, an act that took courage, considering all the opposition they were facing. Zebudah probably heard firsthand about the repair work her dad was doing. Perhaps she even prayed for the work to be accomplished and for her father to be safe.

With so much faith being lived out, isn't it interesting then that later on, when people spoke of Zebudah's son, Jehoiakim, they said, "He did evil in the eyes of the LORD, just as his predecessors had done" (2 Kings 23:37 NIV)?

What impact did Zebudah have on her son's life? Did she share with him the faith she'd seen in her father? Or did she sit idly by and not teach him about God? Perhaps she got discouraged at Jehoiakim's actions and gave up trying to teach him. After all, it's hard to not grow disheartened when we see someone continually making choices that dishonor God.

While we can't force our friends, relatives, coworkers, children, or even strangers to choose God, we aren't without an option. We can be role models, influencing others by the examples we set.

Always, anywhere, each of us can be a light for God.

ATHALIAH: *Limiting Wickedness*

———— ••• ❖ ••• ————

When Athaliah, the mother of King Ahaziah of Judah, learned that her son
was dead, she began to destroy the rest of the royal family.
2 KINGS 11:1 NLT

Wicked Queen Athaliah, the only queen to rule Judah, gained her throne by wiping out all of the royal family, including her own grandchildren; only her grandson Joash, who was rescued by his aunt Jehosheba, avoided destruction. For six years he remained hidden in the temple, with his nurse, until High Priest Jehoiada called together enough military support to crown Joash king.

Athaliah, discovering the coronation, came to the temple and cried out, "Treason! Treason!" But before she could do more, Jehoiada called on the captains of the temple guard to kill her outside the temple. They hustled her out and obeyed their command.

Athaliah threatened more than the lives of a few children. The unbroken line of succession between King David and the Messiah was also at risk, for she would have left no male heir in David's line. But through one faithful woman and the high priest, God restored Joash's throne into his hands. The faith of this king whom God protected led him to restore the temple.

Wicked rulers may cross our paths and affect our lives. Can we trust that, like Athaliah, God has a plan that limits their power and authority? Can we trust that a leader's heart is truly in the hand of God (Proverbs 21:1), and He has the final word?

SALOME: *Be Careful What You Wish For*

··· ❦ ···

The mother of Zebedee's sons came to Jesus with her sons and,
kneeling down, asked a favor of him. . . . "Grant that one of these two
sons of mine may sit at your right and the other at your left in your kingdom."
MATTHEW 20:20‑21 NIV

Salome (identified by name in Mark 16:1 and by her relationship to her sons in Matthew 27:56) had earned the right to ask a favor of Jesus.

When Jesus called Salome's sons, James and John, to leave their father's fishing business, their mother joined other women who traveled with the disciples, taking care of their needs (Mark 15:40–41).

Three years later, they expected Jesus to claim the throne of Israel at any time. When that day came, Salome asked that her sons sit on either side of the throne. With Peter, they were part of the inner three whom Jesus called apart. Recently He had appeared to them in His kingly glory.

Jesus promised that her sons would drink from His cup, but He couldn't promise their seats by His throne.

When, years later, Herod Agrippa had James beheaded, Salome likely still lived. Did she regret the request she made to Jesus?

After her death, John lived to old age. John died, either as a martyr or in exile for the Gospel. James and John bookended the martyred apostles. They drank the cup of the Savior's blood, offered for our salvation.

Sometimes God's answer to our prayers breaks our hearts—but He is always faithful.

JEHOSHEBA: *An Act of Courage*

❖❖❖

Jehosheba. . .took Ahaziah's infant son, Joash. . . . She put Joash and his nurse in a bedroom, and they hid him from Athaliah, so the child was not murdered.
2 KINGS 11:2–3 NLT

Throughout biblical history, royals murdered royal relatives to secure places of power for themselves. In this story, Athaliah, learning that her son, the king, was dead, attempted to murder all his children (her grandchildren) to secure an uncontested reign for herself. Had she succeeded, she would have annihilated the royal line that eventually led to Christ.

The dastardly act was thwarted by Jehosheba (probably the half sister of the deceased king), who snatched one baby boy and hid him from the brutal murderer.

Jehosheba's courageous act led to six years of secret keeping, most likely, six years on high alert. How did she keep the little, growing boy out of view and teach him to be a king? Did she whisper to him as she tucked him into bed, "You are a prince," only to worry that he'd declare at an inopportune time, "I am Prince Joash!"

Her heroic, righteous act led to a long period of stress, possibly endured because she understood the importance of her task. She saw it through. When he was seven years old, Joash was crowned king. God rewarded Jehosheba with success that led to a line of blessing for all people.

When we are faced with tasks that require enormous courage, let's emulate Jehosheba. "You need to persevere so that when you have done the will of God, you will receive what he has promised" (Hebrews 10:36 NIV).

What Did That Woman's Name Mean?

Just as today, some biblical names had meanings. Here are a few of those meanings, including names of some women in this book.

Eglah: Calf

Elisheba: God of the oath

Elizabeth: God of the oath

Ephratah: Fruitfulness

Eunice: Victorious

Euodias: Fine traveling

Eve: Life giver

Gomer: Completion

MICHAL: *Bitter Marriage*

—— ···❦··· ——

Get rid of all bitterness, rage and anger, brawling and slander,
along with every form of malice.
EPHESIANS 4:31 NIV

Michal, King Saul's younger daughter, fell in love with brave, handsome David, who defeated Goliath. Her jealous father agreed to their marriage so she might "be a snare to him" (1 Samuel 18:21 NIV). Instead, Michal masterminded David's escape from her father, telling him David had threatened her into cooperation (1 Samuel 19:11–17).

David's long absence, however, damaged their marriage. Perhaps Michal learned of David's other marriages. With or without her consent, Saul gave Michal to Paltiel.

When David returned, after Saul's death, he demanded Michal's brother restore her to him. Michal had suffered loneliness and pressure from Saul while David was gone. Now stabilized in a marriage, she was commanded to change husbands as she would shawls?

Instead of asking God for help, Michal ripped into David, who danced when the ark of God returned to Jerusalem: "How the king of Israel has distinguished himself today, going around half-naked in full view of the slave girls" (2 Samuel 6:20 NIV). David retorted that God chose him over her father. The Bible implies a permanent loss of intimacy between them: "Michal daughter of Saul had no children to the day of her death" (2 Samuel 6:23 NIV).

Like Michal, we may feel our bitterness is justified, but it only injures us further. If we renounce resentment and turn to God, He will heal us of its deadly influence and restore our lives.

PRAYING WOMEN: *Start with Prayer*

— ··· ❧ ❧ ··· —

*They all joined together constantly in prayer, along with the women
and Mary the mother of Jesus, and with his brothers.*
ACTS 1:14 NIV

It must have been a very scary time for these women after Jesus
died. They had followed Him and been a part of His ministry. They had
witnessed the horrible way He died and rejoiced at His resurrection. How
would they handle life without Jesus physically there with them? How
could they handle those opposing them? How would they live out what
Jesus had called them to do? They would do it by praying.

These women knew there was much to pray for. Protection, wisdom,
strength, comfort, guidance, courage, on and on the list went. They
understood that prayer connects us to God and brings us into fellowship
with Him. Too often, though, when there's an upheaval in our lives, prayer
seems to get pushed to the back burner. We put it off, choosing instead to
seek out advice, read how-to books, and hope that things will improve on
their own.

How many times have you heard someone say, or even said yourself,
"There's nothing left to do but pray"? We need to make praying our
primary response to life's stresses and hurts. Let's adopt the attitude the
psalmist had, who wrote, "O LORD, I cry out to you. I will keep on pleading
day by day" (Psalm 88:13 NLT).

Start with prayer. You won't regret it.

BELSHAZZAR'S QUEEN: *An Important Message*

───── ···❧❦❧··· ─────

The queen. . .came into the banquet hall. "May the king live forever!"
she said. "Don't be alarmed! . . . There is a man in your kingdom
who has the spirit of the holy gods in him. . . . Call for Daniel,
and he will tell you what the writing means."
DANIEL 5:10–12 NIV

Who was this queen who advised King Belshazzar? Scholars are
not sure. It may have been his mother or grandmother, since the word
translated "queen" may mean "queen mother." But when the handwriting
appeared on the wall of Belshazzar's palace, the queen gave him this wise
word: "Call for Daniel." She was no believer in the Lord, as her description
of Daniel makes clear, and she didn't know what the outcome would be,
but she knew of Daniel's wisdom and that he was close to God. Where the
spiritual leaders of Belshazzar's kingdom failed the king, Daniel would not.

Sadly, the news Daniel gave the king was not good. For desecrating the
Lord's temple vessels, Belshazzar's rule over Babylon would end. The king
was killed that night.

God used an unbelieving queen to bring His truth to a proud king,
but she did no more than pass a message on. Are we, like her, passing
God's unopened envelopes to others, or, like Daniel, through faith, do we
understand the holy message inside?

The Gracious Woman: *Reflecting God*

--- ··· ❧❦❧ ··· ---

A gracious woman gains respect, but ruthless men gain only wealth.
Your kindness will reward you, but your cruelty will destroy you.
PROVERBS 11:16–17 NLT

Which is better, wealth or respect? Having enough money is certainly a wonderful asset, but having others treat you with honor is priceless.

Proverbs tells us being gracious produces respect. Graciousness means treating others and ourselves with kindness and mercy. We remember to think before we speak and know our words are powerful tools that can hurt or heal. Being gracious means we willingly go that extra mile when needed.

A gracious woman nurtures respect by focusing on others, not just herself. People will remember how she made them feel and how she was present in their time of need. They will hold her generosity gently in their hearts and minds.

Is graciousness a lost art? Being gracious is a behavior we can cultivate and practice. We can be quick to say thank you and carry out small acts of kindness, like opening the door for someone or being mindful of our tone of voice when speaking to loved ones.

Graciousness softens the heart and creates a place for compassion to grow.

A gracious person reflects God. His grace is the source of graciousness within us. His love dwells within us, so His kindness radiates through us to others.

Jephthah's Daughter: *Celebration Cut Short*

— ··· ❧❧ ··· —

*And she said, "Father, if you have made a vow to the Lord,
you must do to me what you have vowed, for the Lord has
given you a great victory over your enemies."*
JUDGES 11:36 NLT

Jephthah's daughter danced joyfully toward her father,
who was returning home after leading his army to resounding victory.
A horrified Jephthah lamented loudly, "Daughter! . . . You've brought
disaster on me" (v. 35 NLT).

His anguish stemmed from a rash prebattle vow he'd made to God.
He'd promised that in return for victory, he would sacrifice whatever came
out of his house to greet him when he returned home.

When Jephthah's daughter learned of the foolish vow and its
consequences, she didn't beg her father to break his vow, and she didn't
blame him for making it. She encouraged him to follow through.

It seems that Jephthah's daughter saw a bigger picture than that of her
own life. She regarded promise keeping as more important than her ideas
of how her life should unfold.

Often circumstances and other people's actions interfere with our
lives. We can resist and blame, or trust God to work things out. As Joseph
declared to his brothers who had sold him as a slave to the Egyptians, "You
intended to harm me, but God intended it all for good" (Genesis 50:20 NLT).

No matter how we are affected by the actions of those around us, we
can count on God to work good in our lives.

NOADIAH: *Prophetess with an Agenda*

— ···﹩·﹩ ··· —

"Now, son of man, set your face against the daughters of your people who prophesy out of their own imagination."
EZEKIEL 13:17 NIV

Noadiah is mentioned once in the Bible, in Nehemiah's prayer as he and returned exiles from Babylon were rebuilding Jerusalem's walls (Nehemiah 6:14).

Unfortunately, he could not thank God for Noadiah's help. The prophetess had helped Nehemiah's nemeses, Tobiah and Sanballat, disrupt the project.

Why would a spiritually prominent woman like Noadiah align herself with God's enemies? They held significant authority in nearby Samaria and obviously wanted to expand their power base to include Jerusalem. Perhaps Noadiah benefited financially from association with them. Or maybe she saw Nehemiah as a threat to the power she enjoyed as a prophetess. Whatever Noadiah's motivation, she joined Tobiah, Sanballat, and others in lying attempts to intimidate Nehemiah, possibly participating in failed plots to murder him.

Ezekiel, writing decades before the Jews returned to Judah, also encountered prophetesses like Noadiah and spoke God's message to them: "You disheartened the righteous with your lies, when I had brought them no grief, and. . .encouraged the wicked not to turn from their evil ways" (Ezekiel 13:22 NIV). God minced no words in warning these "spiritual" women they would not succeed in their schemes: "I will save my people from your hands. And then you will know that I am the LORD" (Ezekiel 13:23 NIV).

Are we careful about claiming that we know what God wants us or others to do? Or have we allied ourselves with those who might lead us astray?

THE POOR WIDOW: *Two Hearty Coins*

Calling his disciples to him, Jesus said, "Truly I tell you, this poor widow has put more into the treasury than all the others. They all gave out of their wealth; but she, out of her poverty, put in everything—all she had to live on."
MARK 12:43–44 NIV

It's hard to imagine Jesus, the Creator of heaven and earth, being impressed by a widow's contribution to the temple treasury. He must have been, though, because He made a point of calling the disciples over and pointing out what she had done.

What were the widow's thoughts as she dropped in her two copper coins? Did she wish she could contribute a bigger sum, as she saw others doing? Did she have to battle against the "voice" in her head that called her foolish for giving away her last two coins? Were there thoughts of discouragement that what she gave, which was all she had, was too meager to make a difference?

If those were her thoughts, they didn't stop her. Wouldn't it be nice if we were determined in our giving? What if we sacrificially gave of our money, time, energy, and love? What if we didn't let negative thinking interfere in our giving? What if we put God first in our giving and ourselves second?

Jesus wasn't impressed with the amount the widow gave, but by what her giving said about her heart. What would our giving reveal about our hearts?

CANDACE: *Amazing Places*

And [Philip] arose and went: and, behold, a man of Ethiopia, an eunuch of great authority under Candace queen of the Ethiopians, who had the charge of all her treasure, and had come to Jerusalem for to worship, was returning, and sitting in his chariot read Esaias the prophet.
ACTS 8:27–28 KJV

Candace (or Kandake, in Greek) was the Ethiopian queen mother's title. This powerful Nubian woman performed the secular duties of that country's king, who was considered a god and therefore above such worldly concerns. So Candace's eunuch, a treasury official, would have been one of his homeland's important financial men. And though he may not have completely converted to Judaism, he was at least a Gentile who believed in the Lord and worshipped in Jerusalem.

As the eunuch traveled between Jerusalem and Gaza, he read Isaiah 53:7–8 and became confused by it. The apostle Philip, sent by God to meet him right where he was, swiftly explained the passage, led him to Jesus, then baptized the new believer. Though the apostle never witnessed to Candace, his message came to her, carried by her financial guru.

Today, do we fear to tell others about Jesus? God may send the message again, by another, more faithful servant, if we keep our mouths closed. But if we do speak, who knows where in the world God's message may be shared; someone we speak to could pass it on anywhere in the world.

Doesn't that make sharing the faith an exciting prospect?

EVE: *Courage to Continue*

— ···∙⟡∙··· —

To the woman he said, "I will make your pains in childbearing very severe; with painful labor you will give birth to children. Your desire will be for your husband, and he will rule over you." . . . Adam named his wife Eve, because she would become the mother of all the living.
GENESIS 3:16, 20 NIV

Eve's world fell apart. After stealing from the tree of the knowledge of good and evil then lying about it to the Lord, she faced the consequences of her disobedience. God told her she would experience the pains of childbirth.

Adam and Eve started a family, and she did become the "mother of all the living." But even her son disobeyed and committed evil when Cain murdered his brother, Abel. But Eve had another son plus more children. She continued on with life.

Bad things happen in our lives: we lose loved ones, face financial disasters, and endure broken relationships. At times life's unfairness piles up, and we don't think we can face another day.

Eve's name is never given until after her sin. Her identity, her new label, signified she had turned and faced forward to the future. She would now be recognized as a fresh beginning with a new life.

God will give us the courage to persevere. Even in the midst of tragedy, He will lead us forward. Life goes on. Like Adam and Eve, God has named us as His children, and He will give us strength and courage to face the future and continue on.

NYMPHA: *God's Hostess*

Command those who are rich in this present world not to be arrogant nor
to put their hope in wealth, which is so uncertain, but to put their hope
in God, who richly provides us with everything for our enjoyment.
1 TIMOTHY 6:17 NIV

Nympha lived in Laodicea, located in modern-day Turkey, on a major Roman road between Ephesus and Syria. In his letter to the church at nearby Colossae, Paul sent greetings to Nympha and the church she hosted (Colossians 4:15).

We know little about Nympha's personal life, but she no doubt reflected her city: rich, independent, and in tune with the times. Laodicea was famous for its black wool, its banking industry, and its medical school associated with the temple of Asklepios, the Greek god of healing.

Nympha swam against strong cultural currents in becoming a Christian—and even more in offering her home as a meeting place for other believers. During this era in which men controlled most property rights, Nympha occupied a privileged position. She could have clung to what must have been a large, lovely house, but she willingly shared it in the name of Christ. Doing so invited criticism from friends, family, and antagonistic authorities, but Nympha persisted in hospitality that refreshed her fellow Christians.

In our country, we enjoy wealth comparable to that of the Laodiceans. May we, like Nympha, share our hope in Christ and our possessions with generous hearts and open doors.

What Did That Woman's Name Mean?

Just as today, some biblical names had meanings. Here are a few of those meanings, including names of some women in this book.

Hadassah: Myrtle

Haggith: Festive

Hammoleketh: Queen

Hamutal: Father-in-law of dew

Hannah: Favored

Helah: Rust

Hephzibah: My delight is in her

JULIA: *Celebrating Freedom*

—— ••• ❧❧ ••• ——

Greet. . .Julia. . .and all the Lord's people.
ROMANS 16:15 NIV

Julia is listed among the people whom Paul mentions as he closes his letter to the Romans. None of the listed people can be further identified, but scholars believe they were slaves or former slaves participating in the Roman church.

We can assume that Julia knew what it meant to be owned by a master who had the power to completely control her life. She had lived that way. The words Paul uses in Romans to explain the spiritual freedom that Jesus Christ offers must have resonated with her. "The Spirit you received does not make you slaves, so that you live in fear again; rather, the Spirit you received brought about your adoption to sonship. And by him we cry, 'Abba, Father' " (Romans 8:15 NIV).

Although we have not experienced physical slavery, we can imagine the intense desire a slave would have for freedom and the gratitude that freedom would prompt. We can ask God to remind us that we have all been slaves to sin but don't have to be any longer. As Paul stresses in Romans, sin is no longer our master. As Christ's followers, we are freed. We must pursue freedom by obeying God and expressing the intense gratitude of a freed slave.

CHLOE: *Right Side, Wrong Choice?*

---

*For some members of Chloe's household have told me about
your quarrels, my dear brothers and sisters. Some of you are saying,
"I am a follower of Paul." Others are saying, "I follow Apollos,"
or "I follow Peter," or "I follow only Christ."*
1 CORINTHIANS 1:11–12 NLT

Poor Chloe had to deal not only with a church disagreement, but
one that was very close to home. In a time before church buildings existed,
Corinth's church met in her house. No matter what she did, Chloe would
not have been able to get away from the discussions, and how difficult it
must have been to have the entire congregation taking sides right where
she lived. No doubt plenty of heated debates surrounded the church's
regular services. Perhaps some people even tried to get her to take sides.
If anyone was in the middle of the problem, it was Chloe.

Church disagreements can make everyone involved very
uncomfortable. Each believer has opinions, and if many loudly disagree, it
creates an antagonistic situation—certainly one no person would want to
live in the middle of!

When others don't see things our way, how we handle the situation
can be as much a testimony to our faith as the stands we take. Being right
but treating others badly is as wrong as making an ungodly choice.

Let's always treat others kindly, so in the end, God can show us the
direction we really need to head in together.

SARAH: *Learning from Her Mistake*

---

*Then God said, "Yes, but your wife Sarah will bear you a son,
and you will call him Isaac. I will establish my covenant with him as an
everlasting covenant for his descendants after him."*
GENESIS 17:19 NIV

Sarah often gets blamed for a lack of faith when she urged Hagar
upon Abraham. But a closer reading reveals a startling fact: God did not
promise Abraham a son through Sarah until after Ishmael's birth. Perhaps
she felt bearing a son through her maidservant was God's plan all along.

With twenty-twenty hindsight, we see her mistake. But apparently
this was an accepted practice in that era. After all, four of the twelve
tribes—Gad, Asher, Dan, and Naphtali— were born to maidservants.

When God's plan didn't match Sarah's expectations, she added her
own spin. Did she pray about it? We're not told. If she had prayed. . .if she
had waited. . .if Abraham had said no. . .if, if, if.

But once God promised Sarah would be the mother, she believed.
In fact, her faith is held up as an example in the Faith Hall of Fame
(Hebrews 11:11).

Many of us have at least one "if only" in our lives. Like Sarah,
one mistake doesn't end our usefulness to God. If we stumble, let us
acknowledge our error and move forward with confidence.

LEAH: *God Notices Our Misery*

···········❧···❧···❧···········

So Leah became pregnant and gave birth to a son. She named him Reuben,
for she said, "The Lord has noticed my misery, and now my husband will love me."
GENESIS 29:32 NLT

Leah was the older, homely sister of the beautiful Rachel. When
the young, desirable suitor Jacob asked to marry Rachel, no one mentioned
that custom dictated the older sister must marry first. Instead, Leah and
Rachel's conniving father, Laban, tricked Jacob into marrying Leah before
he let Jacob also marry Rachel.

We can imagine the misery Leah had felt all her life when she
compared herself to her sister. Then she was trapped in a marriage that she
shared with her beautiful sister. Leah was unloved by Jacob, while Rachel
was desired and treasured.

When she gave birth to a son before Rachel, Leah found some comfort
in knowing that God had noticed her misery. No matter what causes our
misery, we can find the same comfort that Leah felt. The Bible promises,
"The Lord is close to the brokenhearted; he rescues those whose spirits are
crushed" (Psalm 34:18 NLT).

God gave Leah a son, and she saw that gift as confirmation that God
had noticed her circumstance. We can pay close attention to our lives and
notice the gifts that God gives because He cares for us. As the scripture
declares, "The faithful love of the Lord never ends! His mercies never
cease" (Lamentations 3:22 NLT). When we look for His mercies, we are apt
to see them.

ELI'S DAUGHTER-IN-LAW: *Hope in New Life*

❦

> *When [Eli's daughter-in-law, the wife of Phinehas] heard that the Ark of God had been captured and that her father-in-law and husband were dead, she went into labor and gave birth. She died in childbirth, but before she passed away the midwives tried to encourage her. "Don't be afraid," they said. "You have a baby boy!" But she did not answer or pay attention to them.*
> 1 SAMUEL 4:19–20 NLT

Eli's daughter-in-law lost everything: her husband, her father-in-law, and even the greatest symbol of Israel's faith, the ark of God. All her tangible means of support disappeared; all she cherished ceased to exist.

As she was dying, following childbirth, the midwives tried to encourage her with the promise of new life found in a son. Eli's daughter-in-law chose not to pay attention.

At times our world, too, darkens. Hope is lost: we no longer can touch what we love—maybe a family member, a home, a job, or even our faith. We begin to lose the very foundation of all our beliefs. In our despair we feel powerless, and life seems pointless.

But if we pay attention, God will always send new life. We notice a glimmer of divine light guiding our way. Though the answer may not be what we imagined or bring back the way things used to be, hope eventually emerges, often disguised as underdeveloped and unrealized potential, like a newborn baby.

Faith means clinging to His promised possibilities when everything else seems hopeless. The God of hope will not let us down but will carry us through darkness and bring us to new life.

SERAH: *Important to God*

••• ❧ ❧ •••

And the sons of Asher; Jimnah, and Ishuah, and Isui, and Beriah,
and Serah their sister: and the sons of Beriah; Heber, and Malchiel.
GENESIS 46:17 KJV

Each time Serah appears in scripture, all we learn is that
she was the daughter of Asher, one of Jacob's twelve sons. She had four
brothers. She and Dinah are the only daughters mentioned by name among
the family who joined Joseph in Egypt. That alone tells us that Serah must
have been a remarkable woman.

Serah appears again in the census taken before the Israelites enter
the Promised Land (Numbers 26:46). Jewish tradition says "Serah bat
Asher" was alive at the time of the Exodus. Based on that supposition, she
experienced the growth of Israel from seventy to six hundred thousand
strong. Imagine the stories she could tell!

Whether Serah lived to seventy or four hundred, she draws our
attention. Why is she mentioned in the list? Perhaps her inclusion points to
her father's character. The list also includes his grandchildren when none
others are mentioned. His name means "happy," and he sounds as if he died
well, surrounded by his family.

Like Serah, whether we are only a footnote, forgotten when our
generation is past, or whether our influence remains over the years, we are
important—to our families, to our communities, to God.

WOMEN WHO MOURNED JESUS: *Genuine Worship?*

--- ···◆◆◆··· ---

A large number of people followed him, including women who mourned and wailed for him. Jesus turned and said to them, "Daughters of Jerusalem, do not weep for me; weep for yourselves and for your children."
LUKE 23:27–28 NIV

Jesus was walking toward His death. The crowd around Him was noisy, and one can only imagine the words being shouted as He passed by. In the midst of this group were women who were weeping and wailing for Him. Jesus made a point of telling the women that they shouldn't weep for Him but for themselves and their children.

What caused Jesus to respond in such a strong manner? Did He see falsehood in their grief? Maybe these women were living out this accusation found in Psalms: "You love evil rather than good, falsehood rather than speaking the truth" (Psalm 52:3 NIV). Had someone hired them to be professional mourners who show up at events to cause a scene? Were they there out of curiosity and not compassion? After Jesus died, did these women continue to mourn, or did the tears get shut off and was it back to life as usual?

Jesus can't be fooled by our outward appearances. The Lord knows the motives of our hearts. He sees if authenticity or falsehood resides there.

So today ask God to search your heart and show you where deception might be lurking. Ask Him to help you make the necessary changes so that your worship is genuine.

PENINNAH: *Prickly Problem*

--- ···◆···◆··· ---

It is to one's honor to avoid strife, but every fool is quick to quarrel.
PROVERBS 20:3 NIV

Peninnah married Elkanah. They had sons and
daughters, a sign of God's blessing and a status symbol during their era.

Unfortunately, their culture fostered polygamy, resulting in
competition among wives. Elkanah also was married to Hannah, and
tension ruled their home (1 Samuel 1).

Hannah was childless, yet Elkanah loved her. Peninnah may have
wondered if he would have treated her with the same deference, had she
experienced fertility problems. Jealousy choked all compassion from
Peninnah's heart. For years, she never let Hannah forget her barrenness,
even goading her when the family sacrificed and worshipped together.
Peninnah may have felt spiritually superior, glorying in the gifts God had
lavished on her.

How Peninnah's superiority complex must have tottered when she
learned Hannah was pregnant with Samuel. As Hannah gave birth to
three more sons and two daughters (1 Samuel 2:21), Peninnah suffered
humiliation that compounded the rift between the women, affecting not
only them and Elkanah, but the relationships among their children and
future generations.

Like Peninnah, we may live with painful situations. But provoking
quarrels solves nothing and wreaks unnecessary havoc within a family.
We can choose to take our hurts to God and ask Him to help us reflect His
love. . .or we can instigate quarrels and act like fools.

LEMUEL'S MOTHER: *Instruction for the Ages*

··· ✦ ✦ ···

*The sayings of King Lemuel contain this message,
which his mother taught him.*
PROVERBS 31:1 NLT

Lemuel's mother used her powerful position as queen mother to advise her son, the king, on how to act as a ruler. The last chapter of Proverbs records her advice to Lemuel on how to deal with two temptations powerful men often face, and she reminded him of one obligation of a king. Her advice is still relevant today.

The temptations she warned him against are promiscuity and drunkenness. Avoid that behavior; it is not for kings, she advised. And she encouraged Lemuel to use his voice to defend the poor and needy.

When we find ourselves in positions of power or in positions where we can speak to those who have the power to influence, let's try to speak as humbly and as wisely as Lemuel's mother did. Her wise words are recorded for generations of people to read and profit from.

When we think about using our words to influence, let's pray this prayer: "May these words of my mouth and this meditation of my heart be pleasing in your sight, LORD, my Rock and my Redeemer" (Psalm 19:14 NIV).

And let's not forget the necessity and power of words spoken to encourage people to integrity: "But exhort one another daily, while it is called To day; lest any of you be hardened through the deceitfulness of sin" (Hebrews 3:13 KJV).

DORCAS: *Get Up and Get Going!*

--- ··· ❦ ❦ ··· ---

*In Joppa there was a disciple named Tabitha (in Greek her name is Dorcas);
she was always doing good and helping the poor. . . . Peter sent them all out
of the room; then he got down on his knees and prayed. Turning toward the
dead woman, he said, "Tabitha, get up." She opened her eyes, and seeing
Peter she sat up. He took her by the hand and helped her to her feet.*
ACTS 9:36, 40–41 NIV

As soon as he heard the news of the death of Dorcas, Peter went
to Joppa immediately. Full of grief, the widows cried, telling him of her
kindness and how she helped others.

After praying, Peter said to Dorcas, "Get up."

Taking the live woman's hand, Peter presented her to all the believers.
Ever wonder what Dorcas did next? Perhaps she went back to work,
making sure the crowd of people felt welcome in her home. Perhaps she
woke up the following day in normal fashion, making clothes, being kind,
and helping others.

Dorcas may serve as a role model for those widows and for all of us as
she got up and got going.

We can offer a smile to another, remember to make that long-overdue
phone call, or embrace an interruption as a blessing.

Sometimes we need that extra push to listen instead of talking, to go
that extra mile for someone in need, to be like Dorcas, knowing it isn't
about us but about worshipping God through our service to others.

Let's follow Dorcas and get up and get going today by helping another
child of God.

What Did That Woman's Name Mean?

Just as today, some biblical names had meanings. Here are a few of those meanings, including names of some women in this book.

Herodias: Heroic

Hodesh: A month

Hodiah: Celebrated

Hoglah: Partridge

Huldah: Weasel

Hushim: Makes haste

Iscah: Observant

Jael: Ibex

CLAUDIA: *Faithful?*

─── ···◆◆◆··· ───

Do your best to get here before winter. Eubulus greets you, and so do Pudens,
Linus, Claudia and all the brothers and sisters.
2 TIMOTHY 4:21 NIV

As Paul, a prisoner in Rome, signed off on his second letter to
Timothy, he sent greetings from members of the Roman church, including
Claudia. She was probably an influential woman there.

During the last years of Nero's reign, when Paul wrote this epistle,
conflict surrounded the Roman church. Nero had blamed Christians for
the conflagration that had burned Rome in AD 64, and he persecuted them.
But not only was the church attacked from outside, disagreements within
persisted, too. Concerned about divisions in the church, Paul, who knew
his time on earth was nearly done, warned Timothy to remain faithful in
his doctrine and teaching, instead of telling unstable Christians what they
wanted to hear (2 Timothy 4:1–5).

The pagan Roman poet Martial mentioned a marriage between a man
named Pudens and a British woman, Claudia; some assume that he was
referring to the people mentioned in this verse. Whether or not that's
so, Pudens and Claudia were members, perhaps of some standing, in a
conflicted church.

Today, we may assume that in the early church belief bloomed easily,
but the truth is that ancient Christians faced at least as many trials as we do.
In any age, God does not leave His people's faith untested. No matter when
we live, like Claudia, we must answer the question, "Will I be faithful?"

THE WISE WOMAN OF TEKOA:
Reputation's Importance

••• ⇥ ⇤ •••

So Joab sent someone to Tekoa and had a wise woman brought from there.
2 SAMUEL 14:2 NIV

Joab wanted to do something, to help ease the suffering King David was going through over being separated from his son Absalom. So this battle commander devised a plan to have a woman from Tekoa come to the king and ask for his help on a family matter.

Imagine being this woman. She not only had to remember the words Joab said to her, but she had to deliver them to King David. Was she nervous or afraid? Was she concerned she might say the wrong thing and get herself into trouble or further damage an already shaky situation? Was she worried that if King David found out who prompted her that she'd get in trouble?

Maybe none of these thoughts crossed her mind. Perhaps instead, she felt honored to be picked for this task and believed God would give her the strength to see it through.

We don't know a lot about this woman, but we can tell a few things about her. She had to be trustworthy, reliable, a good listener, and willing to follow directions. She had to be in tune with Joab's mission and not concerned with her own agenda. In addition, she must have had a sound reputation, because that's what Joab's servant was going by when he chose her.

Would our reputation cause us to stand out among the crowd?

SARAH: *A Time to Laugh*

Sarah said, "God has brought me laughter, and everyone who hears about this will laugh with me."
GENESIS 21:6 NIV

"*A time to weep and* a time to laugh" (Ecclesiastes 3:4 NIV), Sarah knew her share of both.

When Abraham answered God's call to follow Him to the Promised Land, Sarah left her homeland, friends, and family. It's possible she never heard from them again. Later, she lost contact with Lot, the nephew who had been like a son to her and Abraham. Most of all, she knew the pain of sterility.

Years—decades—after Sarah could no longer bear a child, she and her husband entertained a stranger who promised she would give birth within a year. She laughed at the impossibility of his promise. A child? To a barren woman?

Something happened after that incredulous laughter. She "considered him faithful who had made the promise" (Hebrews 11:11 NIV). Her laughter turned to trust.

How much time passed before she realized she was pregnant? Did she laugh her way through morning sickness? Perhaps the first laugh came when the baby kicked inside her womb. When she held baby Isaac in her arms, she laughed, a soul-deep sound of faith realized. What other name could she give her child but Isaac—laughter?

Like Sarah, we may have many times to weep, but our time to laugh will come.

LO-RUHAMAH: *Not Loved*

— ⦂❦⦂ —

*And the L*ORD *said to Hosea, "Name your daughter Lo-ruhamah—'Not loved'—for I will no longer show love to the people of Israel or forgive them."*
HOSEA 1:6 NLT

Lo-ruhamah is the daughter of the prostitute Gomer and the prophet Hosea. She is a person in an Old Testament story written to demonstrate that God's compassion and covenant love for Israel doesn't waver or end, despite Israel's disloyalty to God.

Growing up in the household of a prostitute and a prophet must have included less than ideal family dynamics and some tension. However, as Lo-ruhamah watched her father love her mother, she was given the opportunity to see a living human example of God's love: a love that is given unreservedly, even though it is not reciprocated.

Sometimes we have the opportunity to receive such love, often we have the opportunity to offer unconditional love. In fact, this is one of the major callings of the Christian life. As Jesus instructed His followers: "As the Father hath loved me, so have I loved you: continue ye in my love. . . . A new commandment I give unto you, That ye love one another; as I have loved you, that ye also love one another" (John 15:9, 13:34 KJV).

Loving unreservedly and unconditionally is a task that can only be completed when we know and delight in the love God has for us.

PERSISTENT WIDOW: *Heard by God*

— ••• ❧•❧ ••• —

*Jesus told his disciples a parable to show them that they should
always pray and not give up.*
LUKE 18:1 NIV

During Jesus' era, few women whose husbands died inherited
property. Mosaic law assumed families—especially oldest sons, who
received the largest inheritance—would support widowed mothers. Tithes
given to the destitute, gleaning rights, and shared religious feasts also
provided for them. But Old Testament prophets largely preached widows'
rights to deaf ears. New Testament religious teachers may have squirmed
when Jesus told this parable, as He knew their hypocrisy: "They devour
widows' houses and for a show make lengthy prayers. These men will be
punished most severely" (Mark 12:40 NIV).

But this fictional widow demanded justice. Day after day, she begged a
godless judge to defend her cause. The judge did not fear God or man, but
he did fear this widow would drive him insane. So he helped her.

The woman possessed no power but persistence. And persistence
won out.

Jesus contrasted the uncaring judge with His Father: "Will not God
bring about justice for his chosen ones, who cry out to him day and
night? . . . He will see that they get justice, and quickly" (Luke 18:7–8 NIV).

We do not always comprehend God's justice. Often our timetables do
not synchronize with His. But if perseverance convinced the godless judge,
how much more will persistent prayers move our loving Savior's heart?

HAGGITH: *Already Royalty*

••• ✦ •••

About that time David's son Adonijah, whose mother was Haggith,
began boasting, "I will make myself king." So he provided himself with chariots
and charioteers and recruited fifty men to run in front of him.
1 KINGS 1:5 NLT

Haggith, who lived about 1000 BC, married King David.
She was one of his many wives and, because her son Adonijah had many
older brothers, he knew he would never succeed his father as king. Yet he
boasted he would be crowned the ruler.

We don't know how Haggith reacted. Did she encourage and promote
this behavior? Did she try to stop her son's useless efforts?

We do know that both Haggith and Adonijah were already royalty. She
was connected intimately with the king, and his father was the king. They
both already held recognized positions. The lure of more— more power,
more influence, more authority—blinded them to their true roles.

We, too, are royalty. In our prayers, worship, and music, we intimately
connect to the King of kings. Jesus' blood snatched us from death and
the way of the devil and brought us back to God, our true Father. We are
children of God.

We don't need to boast to build up our status. We don't need to try to
make ourselves greater in the world's standing. Our value lies with the One
who is already King and calls us His own. We are already royalty in God's
court.

Zipporah: *A Life Change*

··· ❧ ···

Moses agreed to stay with the man, who gave his daughter
Zipporah to Moses in marriage.
Exodus 2:21 niv

Zipporah had the important job of drawing water from the well to water her father's flock. She and her sisters were doing this when some shepherds showed up at the well and drove the women away. Moses stepped in and came to their defense. He made the shepherds leave and helped the sisters finish their chore.

As she drew the water that day, Zipporah had no idea how her life was about to change. She was now a part of God's plan for Moses, which included marrying Moses, having his children, and going to a land that she was not familiar with. Taken from her comfort zone, Zipporah would face many unknowns.

Like Zipporah, we go about our daily activities when suddenly something happens that takes our lives in a new direction. What's our response to that change? Do we react in fear, anger, or irritation? Or do we respond with confidence because we believe God has a handle on the situation? Most likely we experience a bit of each of these emotions.

When our lives or the lives of those we care about change unexpectedly, it helps to remember God has a plan and the ability to carry that plan out: "I am the Lord, the God of all mankind. Is anything too hard for me?" (Jeremiah 32:27 niv).

You're in God's hands, following His plans. What could be safer?

SHIPHRAH AND PUAH: *Civil Disobedience*

••• ❧•❧ •••

The Hebrew midwives, whose names were Shiphrah and Puah...feared God
and did not do what the king of Egypt had told them to do; they let the boys live.
EXODUS 1:15–17 NIV

The Israelites grew from seventy persons to six hundred
thousand in four hundred years (Exodus 1:5; 12:37). That's a growth
rate of more than 8,000 percent! By the time Jochebed had Moses, births
could have reached as many as fourteen thousand a day. Shiphrah and Puah
most likely represent a small army of midwives who attended births.

Midwives must rejoice in the birth of a child. Although Shiphrah and
Puah were probably Egyptians, they had come to revere the Hebrews' God.
They disobeyed the king and in doing so, won God's favor. He blessed
them with families of their own.

Through the years, others have answered the call to fight immoral
laws. Consider the Underground Railroad and the civil rights movement
in America's history. Civil disobedience doesn't guarantee a happy ending.
Some, such as people who opposed the Nazi regime, paid the ultimate
price.

How do we know we must disobey those in authority over us—
government? Employer? Family? How do we discern the difference
between God's laws and our traditions? What actions does God call us to
perform?

Let us pray for absolute clarity. If God calls us to action, let us move
forward with the same conviction as the two midwives.

DAMARIS: *The Choice*

Some of the people became followers of Paul and believed. Among them was Dionysius, a member of the Areopagus, also a woman named Damaris, and a number of others.

ACTS 17:34 NIV

Paul preached the Gospel at the Areopagus, Athens's highest court, and curious Greeks came out to hear him. Some sneered at him, others wanted to hear more, and some, like Damaris, immediately came to faith.

Acts 17:16 tells us that the idolatry in Athens distressed Paul. Unlike Jews and Christians, the pagans of Greece worshipped many gods. When life went wrong, they tried to figure out which one they had to appease. And if appeasing one god didn't work, they were left trying to figure out who else in a multitude of deities they might have offended. That lifestyle had to be tiring and full of insecurity. And Paul knew it was all a lie. So he shared the truths of God with the Athenians, but no great spiritual awakening followed. Only a few people, like Damaris, understood his message and accepted it.

Still, all Paul could do was offer Athenians the choice. He couldn't make it for them.

That's what God expects of us, too. When we see others heading down a dead end, we can try to point them in another direction. Prayer and a loving message are our tools. Some will turn, while others plow on determinedly in the wrong direction. But ultimately their choice is never ours to make. All God asks is that we point the way.

HERODIAS: *Choosing Death or Life*

— ••• ❧•❧ ••• —

When Herod heard about Jesus, he said, "John, the man I beheaded, has come back from the dead." For Herod had sent soldiers to arrest and imprison John as a favor to Herodias. She had been his brother Philip's wife, but Herod had married her. John had been telling Herod, "It is against God's law for you to marry your brother's wife."

MARK 6:16–18 NLT

Confronted with her own sin, Herodias made bad decisions. Anger led to revenge, and that decision not only affected her but her family and the family of God.

First Herodias married her father's half brother, Herod Philip. Later, while Philip still lived, she married Philip's brother, Herod Antipas.

John the Baptist criticized Herod Antipas and Herodias for their lifestyle, telling Herod their marriage was illegal. Herod threw him into prison to please his wife. Burning with anger, Herodias still resented the correction, and pride drove her to retaliate. The daughter born during her first marriage danced provocatively for Antipas as Herodias plotted to end the life of her critic. John was beheaded.

Revenge never leads to good outcomes; instead, it consumes us and often destroys others. Herodias chose evil and brought darkness to all around her.

Like Herodias, we can choose how we react when corrected by others or convicted of our sins. We all can pick darkness or light. Will we be defensive and attempt to justify our actions? Or will we let God bring our misbehavior to His light and mercy?

The God of second chances reaches out to us with forgiveness. Herodias chose death; God offers life. The choice is ours.

What Did That Woman's Name Mean?

Just as today, some biblical names had meanings. Here are a few of those meanings, including names of some women in this book.

Jecholiah: Jehovah will enable

Jedidah: Beloved

Jehoaddan: Jehovah pleased

Jehosheba: Jehovah sworn

Jehudijah: Female descendant of Jehudah

Jerioth: Curtains

Jerushah: Possessed (married)

LYDIA: *Open Heart, Open Home*

••• ❧ ••• ❧ •••

One of those listening was a woman from the city of Thyatira named Lydia, a dealer in purple cloth. She was a worshiper of God. The Lord opened her heart to respond to Paul's message.
ACTS 16:14 NIV

Lydia was a wealthy, successful businesswoman. The purple cloth she sold was produced from expensive, rare, natural dyes. In ancient times, due to their cost, purple textiles were often only worn and used by royalty.

When the Lord opened Lydia's heart to respond to Paul's message, she extended hospitality and persuaded Paul and Silas to stay at her house. Because she was a Gentile, this visit might have been quite an act of faith on Paul and Silas's part.

Hospitality like Lydia's was an important facet of ancient culture and especially vital to early missionaries who traveled from town to town to share the good news of Christ.

Common practice dictated that a host assessed the intention of strangers and then invited them home and provided food, water, and lodging for guests and their animals. According to custom, hosts provided the best they had to honor their guests.

Christianity highlighted the importance of hospitality. Christ often taught that being hospitable to one of His people was an act of great significance, equal to being hospitable to Christ.

Let's emulate Lydia's hospitality. Her guest, Paul, understood the risks and benefits of hospitality, and he said, "When God's people are in need, be ready to help them. Always be eager to practice hospitality" (Romans 12:13 NLT).

THE WOMAN CAUGHT IN ADULTERY: *Stone Judgment*

...✦...

> *When they kept on questioning him, he straightened up and said to them,*
> *"Let any one of you who is without sin be the first to throw a stone at her."*
> JOHN 8:7 NIV

The woman caught in adultery was being used as bait by Jesus' opponents to trip Jesus up. Brought before a crowd, she stood alone with multiple fingers of accusation pointing at her. Fortunately for her, Jesus knew just what to do to help her in her situation. Calmly He began writing in the ground with His finger. How strange His reaction must have seemed to this woman facing death.

What went through her head as she watched Him writing in the dirt? What do you suppose she thought when Jesus, instead of telling the crowd to leave her alone, suggested that stone throwing could take place if the throwers weren't sinners themselves?

Eventually the crowd dispersed. They couldn't say they had never sinned. Jesus told the woman He would not condemn her and that she was to leave behind her life of sin. He willingly stepped in and helped this woman take care of what she couldn't tend to on her own, her sin.

From this woman's account we see Christ's marvelous grace in action. When we've sinned, we still face the consequence of our actions, but with Christ we don't have to face the condemnation.

Now that's amazing grace indeed!

THE POSSESSED SLAVE GIRL: *The Oracle*

··· ❧ · ❧ ···

She followed Paul and the rest of us, shouting, "These men are servants of the Most High God, and they have come to tell you how to be saved."
ACTS 16:17 NLT

Of all the people who played a role in the establishment of the church in Philippi, the slave girl who could tell the future is often overlooked. Why did Satan compel her to proclaim the truth about Paul and Silas? Did God override the possession with His truth?

Perhaps under the demonic possession that dominated her life, her cries were a plea. *Deliver me. Save me. Put my feet on that salvation road.* Only God knew her heart.

Paul ignored her for days before finally casting out the demon. That led to rage on the part of the owners—their moneymaker turned into an ordinary woman in the snap of a finger. The confrontation landed the missionaries in jail.

Once she was in her right mind, did the slave girl claim for herself what she used to shout? When she lost her ability, did the owners keep her, turn her out, or sell her to someone else?

Something tells us that the Messiah who restored demoniacs to emotional, mental, and spiritual health did the same for her. Whether as a slave, a wife, a member of Lydia's household—she survived.

When we get to heaven, we'll get to hear the whole story.

PHARAOH'S DAUGHTER: *God's Reign*

❖

All the families of the nations will bow down before him, for dominion belongs to the LORD and he rules over the nations.
PSALM 22:27–28 NIV

A baby's squall interrupted the bath of Pharaoh's daughter as she splashed in the Nile River. The angry little cries seemed to come from a basket floating among nearby reeds. The beautiful infant inside won the heart of the princess. She noticed he was circumcised like the Hebrew slaves. According to her father's edict, soldiers should have drowned him.

Her resolve hardened. Thousands of babies had died at Pharaoh's command; this one would not. Her father might rage, but her will would prevail.

While she pondered what to do, a little slave girl approached, asking, "Shall I go and get one of the Hebrew women to nurse the baby for you?" (Exodus 2:7 NIV).

How convenient, too convenient to be a coincidence. But the hungry baby's cries intensified. "Yes, go."

The girl quickly brought a woman who, though impassive at the princess's proposal for the baby's care, cuddled him close. . .as if she were his mother.

Pharaoh's daughter had thought to take a bath, not find a son. But God used her routine to save the life of Moses, who would free Israel from Egypt. God reigned in the life of Egypt's royal princess, though she did not know Him.

He still reigns in high places today.

HULDAH: *Woman of Wisdom*

--- ❧❧❧ ---

Hilkiah the priest, Ahikam, Akbor, Shaphan and Asaiah went to speak to
the prophet Huldah, who was the wife of Shallum son of Tikvah, the son of
Harhas, keeper of the wardrobe. She lived in Jerusalem, in the New Quarter.
2 KINGS 22:14 NIV

When King Josiah begun leading the people of Judah
back to God, one of his first acts was to rebuild the temple. In the process,
the priest Hilkiah found God's scripture, which previously had been
hidden.

Josiah sent Hilkiah to Huldah for advice on the meaning of this book.
Josiah knew her reputation for faithfulness and wisdom. Besides wisdom,
Huldah must also have had courage; women in that culture didn't speak up,
especially to a king.

Huldah was one of many women prophets in the Old Testament.
Huldah focused on God, and, with God's guidance, she helped others
discern the direction for their lives. Most likely, she spent time in prayer
and studied the Torah.

As a prophetess, Huldah listened both to God and others. Yet most of
us have never heard of her. That's because, in the story of Josiah bringing
his people back to God, God gets the glory, not Huldah.

Like Huldah, we can be open to receiving discernment from God and
watch for opportunities to help. With His guidance we study the Word
and find the courage to speak up.

A friend desperately seeks someone who will listen; she wants advice
and thirsts for wisdom. We can listen, pray, study, and help her find the
way, pointing only to God. And, like Huldah, we'll be giving God the glory.

MANOAH'S WIFE: *Levelheaded Mother of Samson*

The angel of the LORD appeared to her and said, "You are barren and childless, but you are going to become pregnant and give birth to a son."

JUDGES 13:3 NIV

Manoah's wife is not named in the Bible. She was childless, and the angel of the Lord appeared to her with the news that she would become pregnant. She was given special dietary instructions to follow while pregnant, because her son was to be set aside as a Nazirite with a special calling from God.

When Manoah realized that he and his wife had seen and communicated with the angel of the Lord, he responded with high anxiety. "We are doomed to die! . . . We have seen God!" he exclaimed (Judges 13:22 NIV). But his levelheaded wife responded calmly, reasoning that God wouldn't have shared the news of the coming son and the instructions on how to care for him, if He had intended to kill them.

Sometimes, those around us react with high emotions, like fear or anger, and our job is to bring a sense of calmness to the situation.

We can be calm in intense situations because we know that God is trustworthy and in control. Let's emulate the attitude of David who said in Psalm 131:1–2 (NIV), "My heart is not proud, LORD, my eyes are not haughty; I do not concern myself with great matters or things too wonderful for me. But I have calmed and quieted myself, I am like a weaned child with its mother; like a weaned child I am content."

DEBORAH THE JUDGE: *A Man's World?*

... ❧ ...

Barak said to her, "If you go with me, I will go; but if you don't
go with me, I won't go." "Certainly I will go with you,"
said Deborah. . . . So Deborah went with Barak to Kedesh.
JUDGES 4:8–9 NIV

A woman might seem like an unlikely person to announce God's battle plans. But when Israel called to Him for relief from the oppression of the Canaanites who controlled them politically, God sent His message through His judge-prophet Deborah, the only judge who bore that double role.

When Deborah gave the battle plan to the Israelite commander, Barak, he didn't ignore or doubt her. Instead he had so much confidence in her that he refused to take a step without her. No one heard a complaint from him about the female messenger.

But often, even today, that's not the case when women have God-given positions of authority. As women, we live in what we like to call "a man's world." We make much of the difficulty of getting a fair hearing from the men in our lives and become irritated when they don't listen to us or they denigrate us.

In actuality, we live in God's world, and He's the one in charge, not people who listen—or don't. When He calls us to action, no one, male or female, can effectively stand in our way, as long as we are walking in His will.

Whose world are you living in?

SHALLUM'S DAUGHTERS: *Soldiers of Jerusalem*

Shallum son of Hallohesh, ruler of a half-district of Jerusalem,
repaired the next section with the help of his daughters.
NEHEMIAH 3:12 NIV

The Israelites who returned from exile took on the task of rebuilding the walls of Jerusalem. Among the list of workers, Shallum's family comes as a surprise.

Shallum was a ruler in the local government. Even in ransacked Jerusalem, a ruler must have lived a more privileged life than most citizens. But Shallum led by example, taking on a section of the wall. Stones had to be moved, measured, cut to size, moved into place, chinks filled— the people spent long hours in heavy physical labor. Whatever their willingness, they probably lacked experience.

Whose hands developed calluses? Whose muscles grew strong? Shallum's *daughters*. Like the judge Deborah and Huldah the prophetess, they stepped outside typical roles for women.

In addition to hard work, they faced threats of violence from Gentiles. Nehemiah split the workers into two teams. Half kept watch, spear in hand, while the other half worked. Shallum's daughters prepared for battle with the rest of them.

God may call us to stay at home. He may call us to build. He may even call us to fight. Whatever God calls us to do, let us take our places with the other members of the body of Christ.

JEDIDAH: *A Positive Influence*

———— ···✦···✦··· ————

Josiah was eight years old when he became king, and he reigned in Jerusalem thirty-one years. His mother was Jedidah, the daughter of Adaiah from Bozkath. He did what was pleasing in the LORD's sight.
2 KINGS 22:1–2 NLT

Judah strayed from the Lord as King Manasseh and his son Amon ruled in evil ways for fifty-seven years. But suddenly the kingdom was being led by eight-year-old Josiah. What good would ever come from that?

Changing an entire country's environment takes courage, guidance, and wisdom. Josiah started his rule at such a young age that people around him had to take a positive influence from his life.

Perhaps his mother, Jedidah, made that difference. Did she take him to the temple to hear God's Word? Maybe she told him God's stories, so his heart would be open to the Lord.

Our faith, too, affects those around us. We are called to do what is right and to be witnesses for God's love and mercy. Our words and actions help preserve the faith and lead others to God.

We have a tremendous opportunity to create local God-honoring and God-loving environments that may eventually impact the entire world. Our faith influences our families and our workplaces more than we may realize.

In small ways each of us can start to make a difference with one person or a small group, but with God's touch the influence could change the world. God's work is accomplished when we focus on the people He places right before us. Like Jedidah, we, too, can be positive influences on those we love.

PHOEBE: *the Woman in Charge*

— ••• ❦❦ ••• —

"Whoever wants to become great among you must be your servant,
and whoever wants to be first must be slave of all."
MARK 10:43–44 NIV

Phoebe is described by the apostle Paul as the "benefactor" of many people, including himself (Romans 16:1–2 NIV). The feminine Greek word he uses, *prostatis*, implies a woman of authority who protects and provides for those under her. Possibly wealthy, with considerable social status in the Aegean port of Cenchreae, near Corinth, the visiting Phoebe is mentioned first in this chapter of Romans that goes on to greet many of Paul's brothers and sisters in Christ.

She could have used her resources to bolster her own ambitions and live in luxury. Instead, Paul also calls Phoebe a *diakonos* of the church at Cenchreae—a "deacon" or "servant." He encourages the Roman church to help her in any endeavors, as she has devoted her life to blessing other Christians.

In the above scripture in the book of Mark, Jesus rebukes His disciples because of their focus on being the greatest. "Those who are regarded as rulers of the Gentiles lord it over them," He said. "Not so with you. . . . For even the Son of Man did not come to be served, but to serve, and to give his life as a ransom for many" (Mark 10:42–43, 45 NIV).

Phoebe, a deacon who served her Master and her church, took Jesus' demands for servanthood seriously.

Do we?

What Did That Woman's Name Mean?

Just as today, some biblical names had meanings. Here are a few of those meanings, including names of some women in this book.

Jezebel: Chaste

Jochebed: Jehovah gloried

Judith: Jew, descendant of Judah

Keren-Happuch: Horn of cosmetic

Keturah: Perfumed

Kezia: Cassia

Leah: Weary

MAHALATH: *A Lonely Outsider?*

❧ ✦ ❧

So Esau visited his uncle Ishmael's family and married one
of Ishmael's daughters, in addition to the wives he already had.
His new wife's name was Mahalath.
GENESIS 28:9 NLT

Mahalath was the daughter of Ishmael, Abraham's son. Esau, one of Isaac's twin sons, married her after he realized that his father disapproved of his Canaanite wives.

We can only wonder what it would be like to be one of many wives. Although polygamy was common in Old Testament times, it seems as if it would be very lonely to be, like Mahalath, a wife of a different people group than the other wives. Would the other wives embrace or ostracize the newcomer?

Was Mahalath's prayer similar to the one the psalmist wrote in Psalm 102:6–8 (NIV), which says, "I am like a desert owl, like an owl among the ruins. I lie awake; I have become like a bird alone on a roof. All day long my enemies taunt me"?

When we feel lonely, set apart from the people around us, we must remember that Jesus knows exactly how we feel and never leaves us alone in our loneliness. In our alone times, we can stick close to Christ. He is the friend described in Proverbs 18:24 (NIV) "who sticks closer than a brother." He will comfort and provide for us. When we are lonely, we can always go to Christ.

ZERUIAH: *Letting Go*

— ··· ❧❧ ··· —

> *Their sisters were named Zeruiah and Abigail. Zeruiah had three sons named Abishai, Joab, and Asahel.*
>
> 1 CHRONICLES 2:16 NLT

Zeruiah's three sons would one day grow up to be powerful warriors in David's army. Loyal to David, they would find themselves in numerous dangerous situations.

When Zeruiah was raising her children, had she thought about where they might go or what they might do? When she found out they were going into the military, had she begged them not to, or did she see their joining as a source of pride?

You don't have to be parents to experience the pain of letting someone go. You may have a friend or neighbor who's moving away. Perhaps you've worked with someone for years and now she's going to a different job. Maybe you're the one who's moving and saying good-bye.

Zeruiah had no idea how the lives of her three sons would turn out. We don't know what awaits our loved ones, either. We can, however, help them in their journey with prayer, support, and a reminder that God has a purpose for their lives: "The LORD will work out his plans for my life—for your faithful love, O LORD, endures forever" (Psalm 138:8 NLT). Even though we don't know what that plan is, we know God won't lead us or those we love astray.

Letting go is hard, but clinging ensnares us. Which action will we choose when the time comes to say good-bye?

RUFUS'S MOTHER: *Loving an Apostle*

--- ⚜ ---

Greet Rufus, chosen in the Lord, and his mother,
who has been a mother to me, too.
ROMANS 16:13 NIV

Did the apostle Paul ever wish he could click his heels together, like Dorothy in *The Wizard of Oz*, and go home for a dose of TLC?

Paul's Pharisee father (Acts 23:6) might have rejected his son after his conversion. Whatever the reason, the apostle didn't mention his parents.

At some point, Paul crossed paths with Rufus and his family. How they met and came to be so close is unclear. But obviously their hearts warmed to each other, and Paul gained a family away from home.

When Rufus's unnamed mother made Paul part of the family, he relished the bond with the woman he described as "a mother to me, too." In her home, Paul could forget his public persona. He could banter with her about the questions mothers always ask: Are you taking care of yourself? And he could receive that loving touch: let me get some meat on your bones. How he must have enjoyed fellowshipping with this family in a way he couldn't with his real parents. Paul treasured her motherly care.

Wherever we stand on the childless to empty-nester spectrum, God may put people into our lives who need—or provide—our motherly touch.

JAEL: *God's Warrior*

— ••• ⟡ ❧ ⟡ ••• —

*"Most blessed among women is Jael. . . . Sisera asked for water, and she gave
him milk. In a bowl fit for nobles, she brought him yogurt. Then with her left
hand she reached for a tent peg, and with her right hand for the workman's
hammer. She struck Sisera with the hammer, crushing his head.
With a shattering blow, she pierced his temples."*
JUDGES 5:24-26 NLT

Jael was a murderer and an assassin. She killed the Canaanite
leader Sisera, who had fled a battle after his defeat by the Israelites.

Cunning Jael offered Sisera comfort and then killed him while he slept.
She took a risk and saved Israel with her strong and decisive action.

Jael made a difficult decision with risky consequences. By taking that
hard step, she ended up being called blessed. With one shattering blow
she fulfilled the prophecy that a woman would kill Sisera.

God's warrior used whatever tool she could quickly find, first the food
in her home and then an ordinary tent peg. Like David defeating Goliath,
Jael overcame her enemy.

This story is not advocating murder or inviting escaping men of evil
into our homes. Instead it reminds us that we, too, have battles to fight in
life. Our enemies are often harder to discern but just as evil.

Like Jael, we use whatever is close by to win these fights. We find
strength in studying our Bibles and power in prayer. We can make difficult
decisions and take risks when we know God is leading us.

We, too, can be God's warriors.

THE CRIPPLED WOMAN: *Know What Good Is!*

———— ··· ❧·❦ ··· ————

*One Sabbath day as Jesus was teaching in a synagogue, he saw a woman who
had been crippled by an evil spirit. She had been bent double for eighteen
years and was unable to stand up straight. When Jesus saw her, he called
her over and said, "Dear woman, you are healed of your sickness!" Then he
touched her, and instantly she could stand straight. How she praised God!*
LUKE 13:10–13 NLT

In an instant, this woman went from being both physically
and spiritually crippled by a demon to experiencing full health. Her back
straightened up for the first time in eighteen years, and her spirit became
free. As joy filled her soul, praises burst from her lips.

But while she praised God, others criticized. The synagogue leader,
caught up in the legalism that afflicted many Jews, took Jesus to task for
healing on a Sabbath day. After all, didn't God's Word say not to work on
the Sabbath?

Some people just don't know what good is! They'd rather follow rules
than the spirit of God's law, and this woman—not the synagogue leader—
certainly had the right spirit.

Not every believing Christian will do things the way we do. Does
that mean we have to rain on others' parades? Or can we rejoice when
God brings good things into their lives and leave Him to sort out petty
disagreements? If not, like that synagogue leader, we may earn solid
reputations as fussy critics, and maybe that criticism will be well deserved.

POTIPHAR'S WIFE: *Looking for Trouble*

———— ···❦❦··· ————

Clothe yourselves with the Lord Jesus Christ, and do not think about how to gratify the desires of the flesh.
ROMANS 13:14 NIV

Perhaps her marriage to Potiphar, one of Pharaoh's officers, did not meet her expectations. If he traveled, she may have endured loneliness. Or maybe she simply was bored.

She repeatedly sought to cross the path of Potiphar's attractive new Hebrew slave. To her annoyance, Joseph avoided her.

She demanded, "Come sleep with me."

Joseph refused. "My master does not concern himself with anything in the house; everything he owns he has entrusted to my care. . . . My master has withheld nothing from me except you, because you are his wife. How then could I do such a wicked thing and sin against God?" (Genesis 39:8–9 NIV).

Enraged at Joseph's continual rejections, she calculated when the servants would be outside; then she grabbed him. "Come to bed with me!"

Joseph bolted, leaving his cloak.

When she screamed, servants came running. She accused Joseph of attempted rape and fed the same story to her husband, expecting him to kill Joseph.

Instead, Potiphar imprisoned Joseph, a relatively mild punishment that made her wonder if her husband believed her.

Did Joseph, when he later rose to power, bring her to justice? The Bible does not say.

But God's Word does instruct us to focus on Christ and to never, ever go looking for trouble.

WIDOW OF ZAREPHATH: *Courage and Faith*

"Go at once to Zarephath in the region of Sidon and stay there.
I have directed a widow there to supply you with food."
1 KINGS 17:9 NIV

When a famine devastated the land, God instructed the prophet Elijah to go to Zarephath. God was going to use a widow from that area to provide him with food. Imagine that widow's shock when Elijah arrived and requested food and water from her.

She told Elijah she only had enough food for her and her son. In fact, the wood she was gathering when she and the prophet met was going to be used to prepare their last meal. Elijah insisted that, if she would allow him to eat first, God would provide food for her family until the rain returned to the land.

It took a great deal of courage and faith for the widow to do as Elijah requested. It wasn't just her life at stake but also her son's life. She had a choice to make: ignore Elijah's request or believe God would keep His word and feed her family.

What is our reaction when desperate times come? Do we close in around ourselves, afraid to reach out? Do we go out and "gather firewood" because we can't see anything but bad days ahead? Or do we believe God is going to provide for us?

At a time when the widow thought life had reached its end, God brought hope to her. He will do the same for you.

THE SINFUL WOMAN: *Loving Lavishly*

"Therefore, I tell you, her many sins have been forgiven—as her great love has shown. But whoever has been forgiven little loves little."
LUKE 7:47 NIV

Simon the Pharisee invited Jesus to dine with him but neglected his duties as a host. Others joined them. Jesus was not so much an honored guest as the victim of a roast.

We're not told the topic of conversation around the table. Whatever they were discussing was lost in the tableau taking place. A woman known for her sinful life had entered the house. She stood behind Jesus, crying enough tears to clean Jesus' road-dusted feet. Who could talk over that racket? She knelt down and unwound her hair, used it to absorb her tears, and washed His feet. When they were clean, she kissed them and poured expensive perfume on His feet.

Who knows what bothered them more, the scandalous spectacle or the woman any rabbi should ignore?

Jesus responded with a story. The woman didn't move, continuing to weep and anoint His feet. Who would love more? Why, the person who was forgiven for the larger debt.

She loved not only because of the number of sins, but because she admitted her sin. She repented, not in words, but in her actions. And she knew Jesus would accept her repentance, rescue her, and forgive her.

Your sins are forgiven. Go and sin no more.

May we follow her example.

MARY MAGDALENE: *An Unbelievable Message*

--- ··· ❧⟡❧ ··· ---

Mary Magdalene came and told the disciples that she had seen the LORD,
and that he had spoken these things unto her.
JOHN 20:18 KJV

After Mary Magdalene saw the resurrected Jesus, she shared
the news with Jesus' followers, and they did not believe her words. Her
words sounded like nonsense to them, but Mary Magdalene remembered
the words Jesus had spoken in which He predicted His resurrection, and
her experience began to make sense to her.

We don't know how many times she insisted to the disciples that
she had seen and talked with Jesus. We don't know how many times they
disputed her words. We don't know how they explained away her message.
We can only imagine the frustration Mary must have felt when her words
of joy and triumph were rejected. Maybe she wondered, in confusion,
when Jesus would appear to and speak with the others.

Sometimes, our messages of hope and joy are dismissed by individuals
who lack faith. We may be tempted to despair or to insist emphatically,
"I know this is true." What we can really count on is that God will use
His Word to its fullest potential. As God's Word, recorded in the book of
Isaiah, says, "So is my word that goes out from my mouth: It will not return
to me empty, but will accomplish what I desire and achieve the purpose for
which I sent it" (Isaiah 55:11 NIV).

DELILAH: *Look to the Future*

---— ••• ❧❦ ••• —---

*Samson fell in love with a woman named Delilah, who lived in the valley of
Sorek. The rulers of the Philistines went to her and said, "Entice Samson to
tell you what makes him so strong and how he can be overpowered and tied
up securely. Then each of us will give you 1,100 pieces of silver."*
JUDGES 16:4–5 NLT

Even people who don't know their Bibles well have heard of
Delilah, the temptress who sold out Samson to his enemies by discovering
the key to the strength of this Israelite judge.

When the Philistine rulers came to Delilah's door, a wise woman
would have sent them off with a flea in each of their ears. But Delilah wasn't
wise or faithful or even in love with Samson. She was a woman of few
morals and little compassion, if her actions toward Samson are anything to
judge by. Money was probably more important to her than relationships,
because it didn't take her long to accept the rulers' cash and trash her
lover's future.

Relationships can be challenging, even for people of great faith. But
God designed us to have them. Money can never fill the empty places in
our hearts or restore our reputations, if we sell others out for it. And what
man would have wanted this Philistine betrayer, after he learned of her
history with Samson?

No doubt Delilah discovered the emptiness of cash the day after she
betrayed her lover, at the very latest.

Can we learn from her mistake?

What Did That Woman's Name Mean?

Just as today, some biblical names had meanings. Here are a few of those meanings, including names of some women in this book.

Lo-Ruhamah: Not pitied

Maacah: Depression

Magdalene: Woman of Magdala

Mahalath: Sickness

Mahlah: Sickness

Mara: Bitter

Martha: Mistress

Matred: Propulsive

PRISCILLA AND AQUILA: *An Excellent Example*

···•❖•···

May the God who gives endurance and encouragement give you the same attitude of mind toward each other that Christ Jesus had, so that with one mind and one voice you may glorify the God and Father of our Lord Jesus Christ.
ROMANS 15:5–6 NIV

Priscilla and her husband, Aquila, are mentioned multiple times in the New Testament. Contrary to custom, in all but one instance, Priscilla is listed first.

Some commentators emphasize Priscilla's name, which is often associated with Roman nobility. The Bible describes Aquila as "a Jew. . . a native of Pontus," in Asia Minor (Acts 18:2 NIV). Priscilla's higher social position could shed light on the couple's prosperity, influence, and willingness to minister to Gentiles.

As a highborn Roman, Priscilla could have acquired considerable education. She also absorbed Paul's teaching when he stayed with them. Later both Priscilla and Aquila instructed Apollos, who believed in Jesus but needed to close gaps in his theology (Acts 18:24–26). Some scholars suggest Priscilla and Aquila—or Priscilla alone—authored the book of Hebrews.

Or perhaps Priscilla simply was the more outgoing. Aquila's gifts may have included behind-the-scenes wisdom and service that complemented her charisma.

Whatever their differences, the two believed in Jesus Christ and devoted themselves to the Gospel and other Christians, risking their lives for Paul (Romans 16:3–4).

Priscilla and Aquila majored on majors and minored on minors. We contemporary Christians, ministering together as spouses or workers, might discover similar success if we follow their excellent example.

TRYPHENA AND TRYPHOSA: *Labor of Love*

··· ❖ ···

Greet Tryphena and Tryphosa, those women who work hard in the Lord.
ROMANS 16:12 NIV

Paul often sent greetings to people in his letters. In the case of Tryphena and Tryphosa, his greeting went beyond a hello. He complimented them on their work. This work that they were doing had focus; it was being done for the Lord.

Work takes up so much of our time. There is housework, yard work, and volunteer work. In addition, we work at our jobs, raise our families, see to our aging parents, and minister to our friends. If we have any time left, we'll work at the hobbies that we enjoy.

Is our approach toward work one that Paul would commend? Would he be able to say that we are "working hard in the Lord"? It's one thing to work. It's another thing to work in a way that glorifies God. Paul's letter to the church in Corinth included these challenging and encouraging words: "Always give yourselves fully to the work of the Lord, because you know that your labor in the Lord is not in vain" (1 Corinthians 15:58 NIV).

God's given us work to do. We need to make a decisive effort to do that work, wherever and whatever it might be, in a way that brings Him glory.

We also need to make sure we're taking the time to thank those around us for their hard work. Knowing you're appreciated can be such a blessing.

SHELOMITH: *Pain of Unbelief*

— ... ✦ ❦ ✦ ... —

Now the son of an Israelite mother and an Egyptian father went out among the Israelites, and a fight broke out in the camp between him and an Israelite. The son of the Israelite woman blasphemed the Name with a curse; so they brought him to Moses. (His mother's name was Shelomith, the daughter of Dibri the Danite.)

LEVITICUS 24:10–11 NIV

Shelomith married an Egyptian who joined the Israelites during their exodus from Egypt. We don't know if Shelomith's husband embraced Yahweh or not, but his departure with the Jews suggests at least a hearty respect for God. Her son must have heard God's revelation to Moses.

Although Shelomith was a Danite by birth, perhaps she and her husband lived apart from the Israelites. When her son came into the camp, he picked a fight, serious enough to evoke a curse. Not just any curse, but blasphemy. The punishment? Death by stoning.

Imagine the fallout on Shelomith's family. Grief? Anger? Finger-pointing? Did they embrace Israel's God with renewed fervor? Or did it push them further away? Did it draw the family closer together or drive a wedge between them?

Shelomith's pain is universal. In the New Testament, Paul warns against partnering with an unbeliever (2 Corinthians 6:14). Like Shelomith, a believer partnered with an unbeliever faces additional, possibly fatal, challenges to a marital relationship.

If we find ourselves in a partnership with one who does not believe, it can bring blessing or heartache. It can tear us apart—or, as Paul also points out, it may lead the unbelieving partner to salvation (1 Corinthians 7:16).

ABIJAH: *Good Examples*

❖

Hezekiah was twenty-five years old when he became the king of Judah,
and he reigned in Jerusalem twenty-nine years. His mother was Abijah,
the daughter of Zechariah.
2 CHRONICLES 29:1 NLT

Abijah (who is also called Abi in 2 Kings 18:2 [KJV]) may have been a queen, but her life was far from perfect. Caught up in idolatry, her husband, King Ahaz, never followed the Lord. He was hardly the perfect example for their son, Hezekiah, and that must have been hard for Abijah, who came from a godly family.

Abijah's father, a Levite who guarded "the entrance of the Tabernacle," was regarded as "a man of unusual wisdom" (1 Chronicles 9:21; 26:14 NLT). Growing up in a family like that, Abijah probably couldn't have imagined what life with an ungodly husband would be like.

Yet despite his father's awful example, Hezekiah became a king in the mold of Abijah's family. He did right in God's eyes and returned his people to godly worship by having the temple purified and reinstating worship there. How proud Abijah must have been of him.

A godly example like Abijah's touches hearts. Hezekiah may have been refreshed by his mother's and grandfather's faithfulness. Walking in their footsteps, he influenced a whole nation for good.

Though we may doubt that our lives could have such an impact, we never know who's watching. Today, whose hungry spirit could our lives touch? It might even be our own children.

JOB'S WIFE: *Curse God?*

---···✦·✦···---

His wife said to him, "Are you still maintaining your integrity?
Curse God and die!"
JOB 2:9 NIV

From Job's wife's perspective, things did not look good.
Physically, Job was almost dead. He writhed in pain. His social life
languished. Those he loved had died or deserted him. Then his despairing
wife added insult to injury by goading him to invite spiritual death.

Maybe we can understand Job's wife's reaction. Watching those we
love suffer is difficult. Maybe she concluded in desperation that a lonely
death was the only way out for Job.

When suffering leads to desperation for ourselves or others, despair
often seems overwhelming. We flirt with ideas of doubting God's
goodness and promises. However, if we refrain from turning our backs on
God, He will help us choose faith.

We can ask for strength such as Abraham displayed, even though he
waited a long time to see the culmination of God's promise. "Abraham
never wavered in believing God's promise. In fact, his faith grew stronger,
and in this he brought glory to God" (Romans 4:20 NLT).

Our faith is not just for ourselves. When we are invigorated with faith,
we can help others see God in their situations. Job's wife would have been
a heroine through the ages had she declared to Job, "In just a little while, he
who is coming will come and will not delay" (Hebrews 10:37 NIV).

EVE: *Debating the Devil*

——— ••• ❖•❖ ••• ———

*"Of course we may eat fruit from the trees in the garden," the woman replied.
"It's only the fruit from the tree in the middle of the garden that we are not
allowed to eat. God said, 'You must not eat it or even touch it; if you do,
you will die.'" "You won't die!" the serpent replied to the woman.*
GENESIS 3:2–4 NLT

Eve should have never even started the conversation with that
crafty, evil snake. We really don't know what led her into this discussion,
but we know the words soon changed her life forever. How events might
have been different if she had taken those questions to the Lord before she
acted on the devil's deceit.

The devil knows how to twist words and confuse us with his lies.
Two-faced dishonesty becomes a clever tool as he coats his stories
with just enough truth to sound right. His skills are the misleading and
deception of humans.

Often simple white lies lure us down paths we later regret. What begins
as innocent fun takes a tragic turn when we believe the misinformation of the
world without coming to God for guidance. We take our eyes from God to
gaze on and crave the shiny temptations around us, and soon we're in trouble.

The devil clouds our circumstances; God clarifies and clears our
confusion. Eve's lesson for us is to step away from deception and come to
God for truth.

THE WOMAN WHO FOUND THE LOST COIN: *Give Thanks!*

"Or suppose a woman has ten silver coins and loses one. Doesn't she light a lamp, sweep the house and search carefully until she finds it?"
LUKE 15:8 NIV

No one likes losing things, especially money. This woman lost a coin. How she responded to that loss says a lot about her character.

She could've said she didn't care about the lost coin; after all, she still had nine coins left. This wasn't her response, though. This coin was important, she decided, and she wanted it back. Instead of feeling sorry for herself, she began searching immediately. She searched carefully, not wanting to run the risk of overlooking the coin.

When she finally found the coin, we learn something else about this woman: she was a thankful person. We know this because she called her friends to come over and rejoice with her.

How do we act when we've lost something? Is our reaction one of anger and frustration? Do we throw our hands up in despair or do we search diligently? Are we thankful when we find what we've lost?

Aren't we glad that when we get lost in the affairs of the world Jesus searches for us? How wonderful it is to know that Jesus doesn't rest until He has us safely back to where we belong. We have a Savior who never gives up on us.

So rejoice and don't forget to invite your friends over while you do.

TWO PROSTITUTES: *The King's Decision*

—— ··· ❧ ··· ——

*He [Christ] is able to save completely those who come to God through him,
because he always lives to intercede for them.*
HEBREWS 7:25 NIV

She kissed her baby's soft hair, almost forgetting she was a prostitute. Her roommate, who shared her occupation, held her own newborn.

The next morning, she discovered the infant by her side had died. But he was the other prostitute's son. Frantic, she found her own baby in her roommate's arms. The woman shrieked, "He's mine! The dead child is yours!"

With no witnesses, the true mother's misery spiraled into despair. God cared nothing for prostitutes. Would King Solomon help? More likely, he would have her and her adversary eliminated like pesky vermin. But where else could she turn?

At the trial, the king's chilling order halted their argument. "Cut the living child in two and give half to one and half to the other."

She begged, "My lord, give her the baby! Don't kill him!"

Her roommate said, "Cut him in two!"

Solomon commanded, "Give the living baby to the first woman. Do not kill him; she is his mother" (1 Kings 3:24–27 NIV).

Hugging her son, she repeatedly thanked the king. God did, indeed, care about her.

Trapped in hopelessness and sin, we, too, may think the King of glory ignores our pain. But Jesus, the wise, compassionate Judge, stands ready to listen and act—if we will come to Him.

ABIGAIL, MOTHER OF AMASA:
Peace or a Sharp Knife?

Absalom had appointed Amasa over the army in place of Joab. Amasa was the son of Jether, an Ishmaelite who had married Abigail the daughter of Nahash and sister of Zeruiah the mother of Joab.
2 SAMUEL 17:25 NIV

When Absalom conquered Jerusalem and Abigail's son, Amasa, became commander of the rebel army, his mother may have rejoiced that he'd gained such a grand position. But before long Abigail would have understood the turmoil and danger that faced her child. Because soon rebellious Absalom was dead, and her son was labeled a traitor to King David.

Then, in one of those twists of peacemaking that changes lives, King David offered Amasa the position of commander of his army, setting aside Joab, Abigail's nephew, who had that job. Again Abigail must have been on the top of the world and relieved that her child was both safe and trusted by the king.

But what a family feud David's decision started! Jealous Joab responded by killing his new commander with a single stab of his knife. A situation that seemed so promising instantly turned to tragedy.

Families are always less than perfect, and some are worse than others. But all of us need to understand, as Joab didn't, that God, not anyone who offends us, controls our lives. How much better it is to bring peace, not a sharp knife, into family life.

LEAH: *Always Less Than*

━━━━━━━━━━━━ ···◆◆◆··· ━━━━━━━━━━━━

There was no sparkle in Leah's eyes,
but Rachel had a beautiful figure and a lovely face.
GENESIS 29:17 NLT

It seems that Leah had spent her life being compared to her younger sister. Each time it happened, she was reminded that she had less: less beauty, less chance of finding a husband. We don't know for sure, but it seems her circumstances—her lack of autonomy, her lack of choice—had brought her so low that her eyes lacked life.

When her father schemed to marry her off to Jacob, who thought he was marrying Rachel, it seems that she didn't protest but rather went along with her father's scheme. Perhaps her position was one of such powerlessness that protesting or alerting Jacob would have made her life even more desperate.

When we find ourselves in undesirable circumstances and lack power to change them, we must ask God for wisdom and the ability to sense His presence in our lives. Sometimes, we can act to change things, and sometimes we must surrender to our circumstances, knowing that our all-wise and loving God is our constant companion. We can ask for confidence that Paul, who endured great difficulty, spoke of: "And I am convinced that nothing can ever separate us from God's love. Neither death nor life, neither angels nor demons, neither our fears for today nor our worries about tomorrow—not even the powers of hell can separate us from God's love" (Romans 8:38 NLT).

What Did That Woman's Name Mean?

Just as today, some biblical names had meanings. Here are a few of those meanings, including names of some women in this book.

Mehetabel: Bettered of God

Merab: Increase

Meshullemeth: A mission

Mezahab: Water of gold

Michaiah: Who is like God?

Michal: Rivulet

Milcah: Queen

EUNICE AND LOIS: *Leaving a Legacy*

―――――― ··· ❧ ❦ ··· ――――――

I am reminded of your sincere faith, which first lived in your grandmother
Lois and in your mother Eunice and, I am persuaded, now lives in you also.
2 TIMOTHY 1:5 NIV

Our roots run deep. Some of us can trace our genealogy back
hundreds of years. Some only know a few bits of information about our
ancestors. Either way, our heritage is our family's story.

Paul writes fondly to Timothy in these verses honoring his devotion.
In a sense, Timothy's trust and belief in God started long before he was
born. Paul recognizes that Timothy's faith foundation began with his
grandmother Lois and was passed on to his mother, Eunice.

What a legacy these women left. They must have discussed what they
believed and explained the importance of God in their lives. Worship
and hearing the scriptures were central to their practices. Their actions in
caring for others must have been evident and their authentic compassion
observed. For Timothy, their way of living demonstrated the path of
serving God and left him strong, secure roots.

Other people observe our actions and hear our words each day. Living
out our faith is a gift we can give to those we come in contact with, and it
becomes an heirloom we pass on. Do they see our practices and know what
we believe? Would they be able to tell others about our compassion and
our willingness to assist those in need?

What spiritual legacy are we leaving for our families?

THE QUEEN OF SHEBA: *Royal Truth Seeker*

"The Queen of the South will rise at the judgment with this generation and condemn it; for she came from the ends of the earth to listen to Solomon's wisdom, and now something greater than Solomon is here."
MATTHEW 12:42 NIV

The Queen of Sheba traveled fifteen hundred miles to see King Solomon, if she came from present-day Yemen, as many scholars believe. If she was from Ethiopia, as others suggest, she journeyed farther. Israel's burgeoning commerce competed with her country's spice trade, so the queen desired positive relations between them.

Her magnificent caravan, carrying gold, jewels, and spices, was calculated to impress even the legendary Solomon.

She could have sent high officials instead. But "when the queen of Sheba heard about the fame of Solomon and his relationship to the LORD, she came to test Solomon with hard questions" (1 Kings 10:1 NIV).

Not only his wealth, but his wisdom overwhelmed her. "Praise be to the LORD your God. . .he has made you king to maintain justice and righteousness" (1 Kings 10:9).

She may have extended mere courtesy to her host and his God, rather than truly recognizing Yahweh's sovereignty. However, centuries later, Jesus credits the Queen of the South with a passion for truth that the Jewish religious leaders lacked.

Despite the current information age, we may be guilty of a similar deficiency. Do we seek Jesus, who is the Truth, with a craving that far surpasses our desire for other treasures?

TEN VIRGINS: *Be Prepared*

"At midnight the cry rang out: 'Here's the bridegroom! Come out to meet him!' Then all the virgins woke up and trimmed their lamps. The foolish ones said to the wise, 'Give us some of your oil; our lamps are going out.' 'No,' they replied, 'there may not be enough for both us and you. Instead, go to those who sell oil and buy some for yourselves.' "
MATTHEW 25:6–9 NIV

Ten virgins waited for a bridegroom to arrive. When he was delayed, the lamps ran out of oil. Half the women had brought an extra oil supply. The rest had to buy more. By the time they returned, the bridal party had gone.

Does the parable mean only super-organized people, like the ones who stockpiled supplies for Y2K, will get into heaven? Hardly, since God's grace covers all our sins.

Several places in the Bible give us glimpses into the Lord's return. Over the past hundred years, people have pointed to the Axis alliance during the Second World War, the establishment of the nation of Israel and the subsequent capture of Jerusalem, and the millennium as signs the Lord would soon return. Today we still wait.

Whatever era we live in, the Lord expects us to prepare for His return. He often sprinkles a few signs to remind us. Without that urgency, we might be tempted to put off witness and ministry.

Let us keep oil in our lamps, as Peter admonishes: "Always be prepared to give an answer to everyone who asks you to give the reason for the hope that you have" (1 Peter 3:15 NIV).

ABISHAG: *No Choice?*

King Solomon answered his mother, "Why do you request Abishag the Shunammite for Adonijah? You might as well request the kingdom for him—after all, he is my older brother."
1 KINGS 2:22 NIV

How much did beautiful Abishag have to say about her future? First she became servant and a sort of human hot-water bottle to King David (1 Kings 1:2–4). Then Adonijah, rebellious brother of the new king of Israel, sent Solomon's mother to ask for her hand in marriage. Insecure King Solomon quickly nixed the idea, since taking possession of this member of the royal harem might encourage his subjects to believe his older brother had a better claim to the throne than David's favorite son.

Hopefully Abishag had not been charmed by the rebel prince, since she had no opportunity to choose him as a husband.

We've experienced Abishag's lack of control over the future in our own lives, when God has taken a choice from us because someone else nabs the job or the guy we really wanted. Just as Abishag had to live with the choice of another, sometimes so do we.

When life doesn't turn out as we wanted, can we still trust that God will use this, too, to bring only the best into our lives? Or will we peer down the years, wistfully looking for what might have been?

MARY, MOTHER OF JESUS: *Praising God*

—— ···◆◇◆··· ——

*"All right then, the Lord himself will give you the sign. Look!
The virgin will conceive a child! She will give birth to a son
and will call him Immanuel (which means 'God is with us')."*
ISAIAH 7:14 NLT

Mary was a young Jewish girl who may, like many Jewish
girls, have dreamed of being the mother of the expected Messiah. When
the angel Gabriel informed her that she had been chosen as the Messiah's
mother, Mary joyfully accepted the news even though she couldn't
understand how the events would unfold.

Despite her questions and despite the pain and suffering mothering
Jesus brought her, Mary nurtured and served Jesus all her life. She
didn't abandon Him when the future kingdom He'd promised seemed
to be dissolving. Mary was in the company of those who witnessed His
wretched death on the cross.

She lived an unexpected and challenging life. Her example and her
words of praise, when the news was announced to her, ring through the
centuries: Mary responded, "Oh, how my soul praises the Lord. How my
spirit rejoices in God my Savior! For he took notice of his lowly servant
girl" (Luke 1:46–48 NLT).

Praising God when life is confusing and difficult may not be our
natural inclination. We may want to complain and chafe against the part
God has asked us to play, but following Mary's example of great faith will
enable us to competently fulfill our role in God's kingdom.

ESTHER: *Celebrating and Remembering*

--- ❖ ---

These days would be remembered and kept from generation to generation and celebrated by every family throughout the provinces and cities of the empire. This Festival of Purim would never cease to be celebrated among the Jews, nor would the memory of what happened ever die out among their descendants.

ESTHER 9:28 NLT

People of the Jewish faith celebrate the festival of Purim in early spring, remembering and honoring the time when God saved the Jews from destruction, as described in the book of Esther. Held as a captive in Persia, Jewish queen Esther spoke out with courage and at great risk to save her people from being destroyed.

Now each year Jews celebrate the festival of Purim and remember this event. *Purim* means "lots." The holiday is named after Haman's decision to cast lots to choose the day when all the Jews in the kingdom should be killed. On this holiday, Jews remember Esther's bravery by reading the book named after her and following its commands to give food to one another and to help the poor. In doing so they commemorate God's grace and love.

Like Esther, when we pay attention to the way God's love and grace works in our lives, we will see His extraordinary peace and forgiveness working through us. We'll remember times when we found strength we knew came only from above. We'll find just the right word to help another or marvel at being there at the right time and place to assist others. Then, just as the queen did, we'll know we've experienced God's guidance.

PERSIS: *A Persistent Woman*

⋯ ✦ ⋯

Always give yourselves fully to the work of the Lord,
because you know that your labor in the Lord is not in vain.
1 CORINTHIANS 15:58 NIV

Persis is mentioned only once in the Bible, but Paul's regard for her echoes through the centuries. A small mystery surrounds their relationship, as Paul, at the time he wrote the Roman letter, had never visited Rome, where Persis lived. Yet, he greets her as "my dear friend" (Romans 16:12 NIV). Perhaps Persis, like Priscilla and Aquila, was expelled from Rome by Emperor Claudius around AD 50 and then returned when tensions eased. Or if a native of Asia Minor, Syrian Antioch, or another area where Paul ministered, she later may have relocated to Rome to build up the church there.

However it was that Persis came to Rome, Paul says she "worked very hard in the Lord" (Romans 16:12 NIV). What challenges did Persis face?

- The huge, diverse city with a population numbering in the hundreds of thousands, perhaps millions, could have intimidated her.
- Rome, though blessed materially, artistically, and educationally, was saturated with paganism.
- Random persecution often threatened Roman Christians.
- If Persis was an upper-class Roman, she enjoyed freedoms denied to other women. Still, overall male domination limited Persis and her ability to share the Gospel.

Yet she determined to serve Christ, regardless of obstacles, sure of her reward.

Let's do the same!

SARAH: *The Beauty of Canaan*

⋯ ✦⟩⟨✦ ⋯

Like Sarah, who obeyed Abraham and called him her lord. You are her
daughters if you do what is right and do not give way to fear.
1 PETER 3:6 NIV

Centuries before Greece and Troy went to war over "the face
that launched a thousand ships," Abram faced a similar problem. His wife,
Sarai, turned heads everywhere she went. She would have been the Miss
Universe of the day. When they fled Canaan for Egypt during a famine,
he begged his wife to act as his sister. She was his half sister (see
Genesis 20:12).

His fears were realized when the Egyptians recommended her to
Pharaoh. God protected Sarai, but she and Abram were kicked out of the
country.

Later, Abraham asked his wife to repeat the same ruse. In spite of her
advanced age, another king added the still-beautiful Sarah into his harem—
with the same result as in Egypt.

Sarah was undoubtedly a beautiful woman who only grew lovelier
with age. She had every human reason to take pride in her appearance. But
according to Peter, she didn't depend on hairstyles, jewels, or clothes for
beauty. Instead, she cultivated a gentle and quiet spirit.

If God put together a calendar of women like Sarah, gentle and quiet,
acting without fear, whom would He choose? Now, that's one beauty
pageant we all should seek to win.

P.S. The good news is He would choose every one of us.

APPHIA: *Filling Our Souls*

Paul, a prisoner of Jesus Christ, and Timothy our brother, unto Philemon our dearly beloved, and fellowlabourer, and to our beloved Apphia. . . and to the church in thy house.
PHILEMON 1:1–2 KJV

Apphia was probably Philemon's wife and therefore had a part in Onesimus's situation, since that runaway slave had been sent back to her household. How the newly converted slave was treated relied on how Apphia, as well as her husband, Philemon, reacted to the apostle Paul's request for leniency.

No doubt emotions ran high in Philemon's household. He and his wife may have reacted with shock when Paul asked them to take back the escaped slave as a brother in Christ. After all, legally they had complete authority over their slave and could even have had him put to death.

Though the couple could have made life very difficult for the runaway, Paul called them to compassion, even hinting that they might free Onesimus and send him back to continue the ministry he had begun with Paul (Philemon 1:12–16).

Like Apphia, we face times when our emotions may edge us toward revenge. Will we try to exact as much as possible or listen to the apostle's voice? Seeking retribution leaves us with empty hearts and spirits. But forgiveness can fill our souls and the lives of those around us.

How will we each react to our own Onesimus?

JEKOLIAH: *Mother of a King*

—— ··· ⟡⟡ ··· ——

He was sixteen years old when he became king, and he reigned in Jerusalem fifty-two years. His mother's name was Jekoliah; she was from Jerusalem.
2 KINGS 15:2 NIV

Jekoliah held a position of honor. She was from Jerusalem—a place of prestige; her husband had reigned honorably, and her son Azariah, who became king at sixteen and reigned for fifty-two years, followed his father's example.

Unfortunately, Jekoliah's son, King Azariah, neglected to destroy the places of idol worship, providing the people with opportunities to worship false gods. Consequently, God smote Azariah with leprosy. Leprosy meant uncleanness and resulted in the sufferer's segregation from the community.

What heartbreak for a watching mother. Maybe, like many mothers, she alerted her son to the wisdom of following God's commands. Maybe she watched in alarm while he neglected his duty.

Jekoliah had lived a favored life, surrounded with success and all its trappings, yet sin crept in, bringing destruction and God's wrath. How did it feel to witness God's discipline of her son?

When people we love make choices that lead to God's discipline, we can resent it, or we can surrender to it. Discipline is painful, but we can accept it because a loving God uses it for a purpose.

"God disciplines us for our good, in order that we may share in his holiness. No discipline seems pleasant at the time, but painful. Later on, however, it produces a harvest of righteousness and peace for those who have been trained by it" (Hebrews 12:10–11 NIV).

What Did That Woman's Name Mean?

Just as today, some biblical names had meanings. Here are a few of those meanings, including names of some women in this book.

Miriam: Rebelliously

Naamah: Pleasantness

Naarah: Girl

Naomi: Pleasant

Nehushta: Copper

Noadiah: Convened of God

Noah: Rest

Nymphas: Nymph given

A Woman in the Crowd: *Being Blessed*

— ⋯ ❧❧ ⋯ —

As he was speaking, a woman in the crowd called out, "God bless your mother—the womb from which you came, and the breasts that nursed you!"
LUKE 11:27 NLT

It seemed like such a sweet thing for this woman to call out, to ask God to bless Jesus' mother. Yet, Jesus doesn't respond to this woman's comment with a thank-you or an "Amen, to that." Instead, Jesus quickly points out that blessings are to be had by all who, when they hear God's Word, put it into practice.

Jesus knows God's Word is powerful. Paul wrote in the book of Romans, "So then faith cometh by hearing, and hearing by the word of God" (Romans 10:17 KJV). It's God's Word that changes hearts and brings about blessing.

Faithfully taking in Bible truths is just part of Jesus' comment back to the woman. What about when He said that we need to put into practice what we hear? If we're not doing that, then we're not getting the benefit of our listening. It's like going to the doctor and having a medication prescribed and then never taking it. You won't see improvement if you're not following the recommended treatment.

We can be thankful that just as Jesus pointed this woman back to God, He does the same for us. Are you willing to read the Bible and put into practice what it teaches? If you do, you'll be blessed. We have Christ's word on it.

ELIZABETH: *A Friendship*

••• ❦•❦ •••

A few days later Mary hurried to the hill country of Judea, to the town where
Zechariah lived. She entered the house and greeted Elizabeth.
At the sound of Mary's greeting, Elizabeth's child leaped within her, and Elizabeth
was filled with the Holy Spirit. . . . Mary stayed with Elizabeth about three
months and then went back to her own home.
LUKE 1:39–41, 56 NLT

Ever wonder why Mary visited Elizabeth and stayed with
her for so long? Perhaps sharing an experience—both being pregnant—
strengthened their relationship.

Or maybe Mary needed the advice of an older, wiser mentor.

Could it be, being pregnant, Mary sought someone she could trust?

Whatever the reason, joy overflowed in their greeting. Elizabeth's
child danced within her, jumping with delight when Mary arrived.
Elizabeth knew the source of that joy—the Holy Spirit celebrating deep
inside her heart when the two of them embraced.

Our friendships can be like Mary and Elizabeth's. We rush to a friend
for hope and encouragement when we are empty. Or rise in the middle of a
dark night to provide comfort to a close companion.

We trust good friends with our exciting and terrifying news. We
listen deeply for hidden hints of God's leading as we share our lives. We
seek wisdom from one another, knowing that in our connecting with one
another God is present.

God's Spirit rejoices when two friends embrace and walk together
through life.

TAHPENES: *The Benefit of Warmheartedness*

—— ···◆·◆··· ——

Pharaoh was so pleased with Hadad that he gave him a sister of his own wife, Queen Tahpenes, in marriage. The sister of Tahpenes bore him a son named Genubath, whom Tahpenes brought up in the royal palace. There Genubath lived with Pharaoh's own children.
1 KINGS 11:19–20 NIV

God brought judgment on Solomon for neglecting the covenant with old enemies. In spite of God's command "do not despise an Edomite" (Deuteronomy 23:7 NIV), Joab, his father's general, sought to kill all men of Edom over a six-month period.

During Joab's witch hunt, Edom's king escaped to Egypt. Pharaoh liked Hadad so well that he gave him his sister-in-law for a wife. The marriage cemented a military alliance.

The families grew closer than ever, mostly thanks to Pharaoh's wife, Tahpenes. As the queen of Egypt, she probably wielded a tremendous amount of power. She brought her nephew into her household. Like Moses so many centuries before, Genubath was brought up in the royal palace, with all the training and opportunities implied by that position.

Time passed, and Hadad learned that both David and Joab had died. He returned to Edom and rebelled against Solomon.

What might have been? If Joab hadn't gone on his killing spree, would Solomon and Hadad have enjoyed peace? If Solomon's wives had formed the kind of extended family that Tahpenes developed, how might history have changed?

Like Tahpenes, let us welcome strangers into our midst—at home, at work, at church.

PRISCILLA: *God's Globe-Trotter*

---

*"Have I not commanded you? Be strong and courageous. Do not be afraid;
do not be discouraged, for the LORD your God will be with you wherever you go."*
JOSHUA 1:9 NIV

Most women during New Testament times lived and died
in the same area. But Priscilla, also called Prisca, adventured across Rome,
Greece, and Asia Minor, planting and developing churches.

She and husband Aquila lived in Rome, but Emperor Claudius
expelled Jews from the city around AD 50. The couple moved to Corinth,
where they met Paul. No one knows whether he introduced Priscilla and
Aquila to Jesus, but their spiritual state and their tent-making business
prospered with Paul's help. Priscilla and her husband hosted a growing
church. But they left all to accompany the apostle to Jerusalem.

However, Paul introduced the Gospel in Ephesus, in Asia Minor,
before continuing his journey. Priscilla and Aquila stayed behind to nurture
the church.

Later, Paul sent greetings to them in Rome and "the church that meets
at their house" (Romans 16:3–5 NIV), so the pair must have returned to that
city when tensions waned. But Priscilla may have kept her suitcase packed,
for Paul, in his last letter to Timothy in Ephesus, greeted the couple there (2
Timothy 4:19).

Despite challenging travel and persecution, Priscilla welcomed people
of many backgrounds to her home. Always seeking exciting new horizons
where she could spread the Gospel, Priscilla never suffered from boredom.

We don't have to, either!

DINAH: *Invisible, Vulnerable, and Voiceless*

Later she gave birth to a daughter and named her Dinah.
GENESIS 30:21 NLT

Dinah lived overshadowed by twelve brothers, the only girl in her family. Her birth came right before Joseph was born, Jacob's favorite son. Did Jacob ever notice her? Since she was "only a girl," she probably held little value.

Except for one incident in Genesis 34, the Bible doesn't give us many details about Dinah. When she was raped, she suddenly had some importance. Her brothers, angry because the family name was ruined, took revenge. Still, though we learn of their violent reaction, we never learn what happened to Dinah.

As a woman, Dinah is invisible in her vulnerability and voiceless in her own story.

Women today still are invisible, vulnerable, and voiceless. We don't hear the cries of women in other countries. We avoid the parking lots in our own communities where women sell themselves. We turn off the news when reports of unjust violence occur throughout the world or even in our own backyard.

But nobody is invisible to God. He sees each one of us, including those victimized by society and circumstance.

In our vulnerability, God stands with us, giving us courage to take a stand and make a difference.

God gives each of us a voice to speak for the voiceless. He awakens our awareness of injustice and inspires us to consider what positive action we can take to correct wrongs.

Dinah may have been invisible, vulnerable, and voiceless, but with God's help, we don't have to be.

THE WITCH OF ENDOR: *Unlikely Tool*

Saul then said to his attendants, "Find me a woman who is a medium,
so I may go and inquire of her."
1 SAMUEL 28:7 NIV

Saul was about to do battle with the Philistines and needed assistance. He inquired of the Lord of how things would go, but the Lord didn't answer him. Desperate, Saul asked to speak to a medium.

Saul arrived at the witch of Endor's house in disguise. The woman didn't want to grant his request. She said helping him would lead to her death, because Saul had cut off the mediums. Saul insisted she'd be safe. Finally, she granted his request. Unfortunately for Saul, the news he got from Samuel wasn't good. Upon seeing his distress, this woman encouraged Saul to stay and eat something before departing from her home.

Do you find it a bit strange that God chose to work through this woman spiritualist whose beliefs were so against His law? Why would He pick her, knowing what she was like? When we come to puzzling passages like this it's good to remember this verse: " 'My thoughts are nothing like your thoughts,' says the LORD. 'And my ways are far beyond anything you could imagine' " (Isaiah 55:8 NLT).

God's capable of using the most unlikely people to carry out His plans. This is great news for us because it means that despite all our imperfections and mistakes, God still wants us to play a part in His plans.

Isn't that amazing?

DEBORAH THE JUDGE: *What's Your Song?*

On that day Deborah and Barak son of Abinoam sang this song: "When the princes in Israel take the lead, when the people willingly offer themselves-- praise the LORD! Hear this, you kings! Listen, you rulers! I, even I, will sing to the LORD; I will praise the LORD, the God of Israel, in song."

JUDGES 5:1–3 NIV

When Israel gained the victory over Jabin, king of Canaan, the Israelites' judge and commander knew where success came from. The willingness of the nation to seek God for deliverance and follow where God led had won the battle, not the quality of the arms Israelite soldiers wielded or the wisdom of their commanders. Accordingly, following the destruction of Jabin and the freeing of their nation, both Judge Deborah, and Commander Barak publically sang praises to the One who had led them to victory. Together they retold the story of Judges 4 in song and praised Jael, who took the life of the Canaanite commander, Sisera. Though they sang of their own parts in the victory, Deborah and Barak made it even more apparent that God got the real glory.

When we pray and God answers with some good thing in our lives, do we immediately grab the credit for it? Or do we understand who was really behind the new gift in our lives or the overcoming of that obstacle? When we recognize His hand working through us, will others hear our praise to the Lord who made it happen? Or will we sing our own praises instead?

SAPPHIRA: *Partner in Crime*

*With his wife's full knowledge he kept back part of the money for himself,
but brought the rest and put it at the apostles' feet.*

ACTS 5:2 NIV

"Ananias and Sapphira." The names are always mentioned together, like "Bonnie and Clyde." We remember both couples for their crimes and the manner of their deaths.

Why did God strike Ananias and Sapphira dead for lying about how much money they received for the property they sold? We don't know. What is clear is that both husband and wife were held accountable. Sapphira knew the details of the transaction, but she stayed at home while Ananias presented their offering. Three hours later, she arrived at the assembly. Perhaps she expected a grateful welcome. Instead, she saw no sign of her husband. Before she could wonder why, Peter asked her a single question: "Is this the amount of money you received?"

Confidently, carefully coached, she said, "Yes." She died in the same manner as her husband.

Sapphira had a choice. She could have objected when Ananias sold the land. She could have begged him to give all the money to the church, instead of holding some back. She could have refused to lie about it. When Peter asked her directly, she could have told the truth. Instead, she committed the same sins as her husband.

In Christ, "there is neither male nor female" (Galatians 3:28 KJV). We can't say, "I was just following orders." The choice is ours.

JEZEBEL: *And Then There Was Nothing*

---

*"Jezebel's body will be like dung on the ground in the plot at Jezreel,
so that no one will be able to say, 'This is Jezebel.'"*
2 KINGS 9:37 NIV

In life, Jezebel commanded notice. Her reputation, due to treachery and evil influence, was far reaching and fear inducing. For example, when Jezebel threatened, God's servant Elijah ran, hid, and thought about giving up his ministry and life.

After her brutal death, nothing of note remained. There was little physical evidence to indicate that Jezebel had lived. She was thrown to the ground, and horses trampled her, leaving only parts of her body to bury or mark. Her raging presence was extinguished.

Humans show regard for a person's life by caring for that person's remains and speaking of his or her noteworthy acts. Jezebel's punishment, in addition to her brutal death, was that there would be no way for her remains to be cared for.

Jezebel's end can prompt us to consider the mark that we will eventually leave here on earth. Do we want to leave wealth? A stellar reputation? More than that?

Because we seek to live a life with eternal significance, a life that God notices, we "set [our] hearts on things above, where Christ is, seated at the right hand of God" (Colossians 3:1 NIV).

Life lived with its physical end in view can help us to prioritize our values and focus on things that matter.

NAOMI: *Empty Cup?*

•••◆•◆•••

Weeping may stay for the night, but rejoicing comes in the morning.
PSALM 30:5 NIV

"The Lord's hand has gone out against me!" Naomi cried.

Perhaps she believed He was punishing her family for moving from Israel to Moab, whose people continually influenced hers to follow other gods. Naomi's husband, Elimelech, died. Her sons, Mahlon and Kilion, married Moabite women, Ruth and Orpah, but died childless. As males provided the sole security for a woman of that era, grieving Naomi could not imagine anything worse. Had God forsaken her because her sons took pagan wives?

Naomi's inner compass pointed her toward a return to Israel. She told her daughters-in-law to go back to their parents. "May the LORD show you kindness, as you have shown kindness to your dead husbands and to me" (Ruth 1:8 NIV).

Ruth and Orpah wanted to accompany Naomi, but she believed their only hope rested in finding new husbands. Reluctantly Orpah kissed Naomi good-bye, but Ruth balked: "Your people will be my people and your God my God" (Ruth 1:16 NIV).

Wearily, Naomi gave in. When they arrived in Bethlehem, she told her friends the Lord had wreaked havoc in her life. Grief clouded her ability to see His provision in Ruth's love. In Naomi's mind, her cup was not just half empty. Death had drained it to the dregs.

Like Naomi, we may doubt God loves us. But He planned special blessings for her. And He stands ready to fill our cups, too.

What Did That Woman's Name Mean?

Just as today, some biblical names had meanings. Here are a few of those meanings, including names of some women in this book.

Orpah: Mane

Peninnah: A pearl, round

Phoebe: Bright

Puah: A blast

Rachel: Ewe

Rahab: Proud

Rebekah: Fettering by beauty

Reumah: Raised

THE SYROPHENICIAN WOMAN:
Humbleness before God

— ···✦◇✦··· —

*And, behold, a woman of Canaan came out of the same coasts, and cried
unto him, saying, Have mercy on me, O Lord, thou son of David;
my daughter is grievously vexed with a devil. But he answered her not a word.*
MATTHEW 15:22–23 KJV

The Syrophenician woman had a problem: her daughter was
possessed by a demon, which tortured her without mercy. This woman's
quest for her daughter's healing took her to the feet of Jesus.

What boldness it took for her to approach Jesus the way she did. At
first Jesus did not answer the woman's pleas for help. His silence did not
deter her. She kept asking until finally the disciples, tired of her begging,
asked Jesus to send her away.

Jesus didn't respond with an immediate yes. It's here that we see
another quality this woman had, humbleness. She saw her "place" in the
world, and she wasn't bitter over it. Peter tells us, "Humble yourselves
therefore under the mighty hand of God, that he may exalt you in due time"
(1 Peter 5:6 KJV).

How do we come to God? Do we come with puffed-up hearts? Do we
come with a feeling that we're entitled to something? Or perhaps we're
afraid to even bring our requests before God.

We should never let fear stop us from seeking God. Bold is okay, as
long as it's on a pair of bent knees.

ELISHEBA: *Family Pedigree and Problems*

— ••• ◆•◆ ••• —

Aaron married Elisheba, the daughter of Amminadab and sister of Nahshon,
and she gave birth to his sons, Nadab, Abihu, Eleazar, and Ithamar.
EXODUS 6:23 NLT

Aaron and Elisheba had four sons. What a great start to
life, being raised by the spokesperson of Moses and the high priest of
the Israelites. Though their birthright opened doors for them to serve as
priests, being born into a good family offered no guarantee against poor
decisions and heartbreak.

We learn in Leviticus 10 that two of the sons, Nadab and Abihu,
made offerings to God in a wrongful manner. They died because of their
disobedience to God.

The two remaining sons, Eleazar and Ithamar, followed God and
certainly made their parents proud. They both served as priests, and, when
Aaron died, Eleazar became high priest in his place. Elisheba and Aaron's
other son, Ithamar, was given command of all the Levites.

We don't know much about Elisheba and barely take notice of her role.
Elisheba faced triumph as well as heartache. We can imagine, though, she
worked with her husband, doing her best to raise sons that would serve
God. Her life honored God in a very quiet, behind-the-scenes way that
made an impact on the future.

Even in times of our own heartache, we are called to obey God.
We, too, can serve God in private and nonpublic acts of kindness. Like
Elisheba, our small deeds carry huge weight in changing the world.

REBEKAH: *Strength Taken to the Extreme*

So she quickly emptied her jar into the trough, ran back to the well to draw more water, and drew enough for all his camels.

GENESIS 24:20 NIV

Abraham's servant Eliezer prayed for a wife for his master's heir—prayers that were answered when Rebekah arrived at the well. A camel can drink more than 160 gallons of water a day. Even with a gallon bucket in each hand, that requires eighty trips from well to trough for each camel. She completed the backbreaking, blister-causing, day-wasting job entirely by herself.

Years later, underneath her lined and leathered skin, Rebekah's propensity for extreme measures hadn't changed. The future of her favorite son—not to mention the son God had chosen—was at risk. Rebekah concocted a scheme more audacious than watering many camels. Dress quiet Jacob in his brother, Esau's, clothes and strap animal hides to his arms and legs. Trick his blind father into giving him the blessing Isaac intended to give to Esau.

When it came to Eliezer, Rebekah demonstrated the strength of going to the extreme. By blessing a stranger, she became one of Israel's matriarchs.

But strengths turned inside out become weaknesses. When Jacob's position as Rebekah's favorite and God's chosen one was threatened, her choice tore her family apart. She never saw Jacob again.

Like her, we may push our strengths over the edge. Let's ask God to keep us in balance.

DELILAH: *Queen of Dysfunction*

—— ··· ❧ ··· ——

Then Delilah pouted, "How can you tell me, 'I love you,' when you don't share your secrets with me? You've made fun of me three times now, and you still haven't told me what makes you so strong!"
JUDGES 16:15 NLT

Delilah was the queen of dysfunctional sexual relationships, as we can tell by her interaction with Samson. Caught out three times, trying to discover the secret of her lover's strength, she turned the tables on Samson, blaming him for everything. Trapped in her accusations, the strong man didn't even begin to worry that she might cause him harm. This temptress must have had the Jewish strong man caught firmly in her net.

Nothing about this couple's relationship seems healthy. It's filled with selfishness, manipulation, lust, and greed, and all those things led them straight into disaster.

God doesn't want us to suffer from such tortured relationships as Samson and Delilah's, so He provides us with better ways to relate to others. As we draw near to Him and obey His Word, our ability to resist sin improves, our love for others and for our Lord grows, and our dysfunction levels decrease. Though they may not be perfect, we begin to have the kind of relationships He designed humans to enjoy and thrive in.

Today, are we taking relationship guidance from the Lord? He has plenty to offer. It's all right there in His Word.

MARY MAGDALENE: *A Free Woman*

* ❧ ❧ *

After Jesus rose from the dead early on Sunday morning, the first person who saw him was Mary Magdalene, the woman from whom he had cast out seven demons.

MARK 16:9 NLT

Jesus meets us at our place of greatest need, as Mary Magdalene's experience demonstrates. Jesus met Mary in her broken life and cast seven demons from her, changing her life. Then God used her life to fulfill promises that He had mentioned again and again throughout history; she became living proof of Jesus' power to change lives. Through her, people could see God fulfilling Isaiah's prophecy that He would "let the oppressed go free, and remove the chains that bind people" (Isaiah 58:6 NLT).

Jesus had removed Mary Magdalene's spiritual chains, and she responded with love, devotion, and service. Even in her grief and dashed hope, following Jesus' death, she was up before sunrise on the Sunday after Jesus' death and on her way to His tomb. She planned to anoint Jesus' body with spices as an act of devotion and love; she was not expecting His resurrection.

But the story doesn't end there. Jesus met Mary in her overwhelming grief and let her be the first person to glimpse the resurrection proof of His victory over death, so that she could spread the message of victory and joy: "Thanks be to God, who delivers me through Jesus Christ our Lord!" (Romans 7:25 NIV).

Not only did Jesus fulfill that promise in Mary's life, He's willing to fulfill it for us all.

ZILPAH: *Caught in the Middle*

When Leah saw that she had stopped having children,
she took her servant Zilpah and gave her to Jacob as a wife.
GENESIS 30:9 NIV

Jacob was a man wanted by two sisters, Rachel and Leah.
Rachel was the woman Jacob loved and chose to marry. Leah was the one
he'd been tricked into marrying. Caught up in the middle of this sibling
rivalry was Zilpah.

Zilpah was Leah's maidservant, and as such, she had little input in
how her life would be led. The competition between Rachel and Leah to
give Jacob children was so fierce that Leah gave Zilpah to Jacob. Zilpah
would become his wife and bear his children, children that she wouldn't
even be able to name. Had Leah spoken kindly to Zilpah and prepared her
for this role she was about to take on? Or did she handle Zilpah as a piece
of property, with no regard to her feelings?

We may find ourselves in the middle of someone else's conflict. Or
maybe we're unwitting pawns, seen as nothing more than the means to an
end. When that happens, remember that while people's motives toward us
may be self-serving, God's never are.

As Joseph told his brothers, "You intended to harm me, but God
intended it for good to accomplish what is now being done" (Genesis
50:20 NIV).

Being caught in the middle isn't a comfortable place to be, but with
God beside us, it isn't a solitary place.

MARY OF BETHANY: *Faithfully Forgetful*

— ⋯ ⟡ ⋯ —

Jesus replied: " 'Love the Lord your God with all your heart
and with all your soul and with all your mind.' "
MATTHEW 22:37 NIV

Mary peered out the window again. Jesus was returning to
Bethany, despite its proximity to Jerusalem, where religious leaders sought
His life. Would they succeed? Mary shuddered and focused on the joy of
seeing Jesus. She longed to sit at His feet again, listening and learning. This
time, she did not think Martha would object.

When His party arrived, Jesus looked thin and weary. Mary
determined a plan to assure Him of her love.

A dinner was given in Jesus' honor. Women guests were not welcome.
Still, grasping an elegant alabaster jar of perfume, Mary took a deep breath
and entered.

Conversation ceased. Bearded faces glared, but Mary fastened her gaze
on Jesus as she stepped between reclining bodies. Breaking the jar, Mary
poured perfume on His head, His feet. Its fragrance saturated the room.

Judas sneered, "That could have been sold for a year's wages, the
money given to the poor!"

A murmur of angry assent rumbled to a roar when Mary removed her
veil and wiped Jesus' feet with her hair.

"Leave her alone."

Only a few words. But they quelled the storm of criticism.

Jesus declared, "She has done a beautiful thing to me" (Mark 14:6 NIV).

He welcomed her worship. Mary forgot everything and everyone else,
including herself. She saw only Jesus.

Oh, that we could be forgetful as well.

THE SHULAMMITE: *Burning Love*

— ··· ❧ ··· —

Place me like a seal over your heart. . .for love is as strong as death. . . .
It burns like blazing fire. . . . Many waters cannot quench love; rivers
cannot sweep it away. If one were to give all the wealth of one's house
for love, it would be utterly scorned.
SONG OF SOLOMON 8:6–7 NIV

Love is a burning thing. Perhaps June Carter Cash was thinking of Solomon's words when she penned her highly popular song, "Ring of Fire." She certainly knew that truth, with her chaotic, lifelong romance with Johnny Cash.

The Song of Solomon describes love in similar words. Taking the text at face value and not as an allegory of Christ and the church, we read a passionate love story. The Shulammite asked Solomon to seal her to his heart. Her love burned too strong for the best firefighting equipment to douse it.

His lyrical response sounds like a lovesick teenager. Unfortunately Solomon didn't stay committed to any woman for long, with three hundred wives and seven hundred concubines. The wealth of her heart and her dowry, given willingly, ultimately was scorned.

God loves us with that kind of passionate love, one that is "as strong as death." He sent His own Son to die—and called Him back from the grave three days later.

God gives us burning love to warm us, to arm us against harm, to motivate us to action. Nothing in all creation can separate us from that love. Let us take refuge in His ring of fire.

THE FOOLISH WOMAN: *Don't Tear Down, Build Up*

- ••• ❧❧ ••• -

The wise woman builds her house,
but with her own hands the foolish one tears hers down.
PROVERBS 14:1 NIV

Proverbs can be a tough read. This book full of wisdom also sends us uncomfortable and challenging warnings. It is easy to skim over these verses, ignore them, or pretend the words don't apply to us. But if we are honest, the lessons in Proverbs correct and guide us even today.

How are we building our homes and our lives?

This verse warns us that the foolish woman destroys her home with her own hands. By her own means, she sabotages all the good she has built and demolishes the things she values.

Though it's a harsh reality to accept, most of our own problems come from inside of us and are not caused by others. We find it much easier to blame society, blame our family, and blame our circumstances.

Then we give up, saying we can't change or we will never change. The truth is that it is through our own hands we tear down the home of our hearts.

But our own hands can also be folded in prayer. We can give our foolish ways to God, who will help us build a new home. We can restore our hearts to be a place of strength, understanding, and love.

Today let's empty our hands of all our foolish ways and ask the God of wisdom to help us build up, not tear down.

BATHSHEBA: *A Matter of Influence*

······ ❧·❧ ······

Nathan asked Bathsheba, . . . "Have you not heard that Adonijah. . .has become king, and our lord David knows nothing about it? . . . Let me advise you how you can save your own life and the life of your son Solomon. Go in to King David. . . . While you are still there talking to the king, I will come in and add my word to what you have said."
1 KINGS 1:11–14 NIV

Bathsheba lived in a political world filled with powerful men. But when the prophet Nathan saw a danger to Israel's succession, he bypassed the men and came to her. The wise prophet knew the influence she had with David, and obviously he had compassion for her and her son. After coaching her on what to say, Nathan threw his support behind David's wife.

Bathsheba went to the king, reminded him he'd promised Solomon the throne, and told him that his son Adonijah had grabbed it instead. Then Nathan entered and updated the ailing king on the latest news of Adonijah's actions. David immediately believed their account and supported Solomon as his heir.

Though Bathsheba had powerful influence and had been part of the court for many years, she was not too proud to accept advice from a man of God who had her best interests at heart. Can we do the same? Or will our own sense of self-importance keep us from hearing God's word to us?

What Did That Woman's Name Mean?

Just as today, some biblical names had meanings. Here are a few of those meanings, including names of some women in this book.

Rhoda: Rose

Rizpah: Hot stone

Ruth: Friend

Sapphira: Sapphire

Sarah: Female noble

Sarai: Controlling

Serah: Superfluity

Shelomith: Peaceableness

MAHLAH, NOAH, HOGLAH, MILCAH, AND TIRZAH:
Desirable Mention

*** ❦ ***

*And Zelophehad the son of Hepher had no sons, but daughters:
and the names of the daughters of Zelophehad were Mahlah,
and Noah, Hoglah, Milcah, and Tirzah.*
NUMBERS 26:33 KJV

In Old Testament times, women did not enjoy equal social
standing with men. Usually only men's names were recorded in biblical
genealogies, but in this census of the Israelites the five daughters of
Zelophehad, Mahlah, Noah, Hoglah, Milcah, and Tirzah, are named.

This is probably due to the fact that Zelophehad did not have sons,
but also because in God's kingdom, women have worth. The Bible makes
clear that regardless of one's gender, the terms of essential spiritual worth
are the same. We are worthwhile because we are children of God. As
John reminds us in 1 John 3:1 (NLT), "See how very much our Father loves
us, for he calls us his children, and that is what we are!" According to
Galatians 3:26–29, as believers, we are all equal under God and receive His
inheritance.

Because, as God's children, we are worthwhile, whether we are
male or female, He has written our names in an eternal document that is
mentioned in Revelation 21:27. John describes the eternal kingdom of God
and says, "Nothing evil will be allowed to enter, nor anyone who practices
shameful idolatry and dishonesty—but only those whose names are written
in the Lamb's Book of Life" (NLT).

ZIBIAH: *A Story Passed Down to Others*

··· ❦ ···

In the seventh year of Jehu, Joash became king, and he reigned in Jerusalem forty years. His mother's name was Zibiah; she was from Beersheba.

2 KINGS 12:1 NIV

Imagine being mother to a king. What type of influence did Zibiah have on her son? It would seem it was a positive one, given that Joash's actions, during the forty years he ruled, pleased God. How might she have come by such strong wisdom and instructions? Perhaps it came from where she came from.

Beersheba is mentioned over thirty times in the Bible. Across Beersheba's terrain walked such biblical "giants" as Jacob, Isaac, and Abraham, who give this area its name and made it a place of worship: "Then Abraham planted a tamarisk tree at Beersheba, and there he worshipped the LORD, the Eternal God" (Genesis 21:33 NLT).

Being from Beersheba, Zibiah probably heard stories of these men and their faithfulness. Perhaps she passed these stories on to her son, allowing for another generation to hear about God's mercy and grace.

Sharing what God has done in our lives should be an honor. Too often, though, we let fear or shyness or the thought that no one cares hold us back. We must work to fight off our fears and doubts, because the story of God's grace in our life may be just the thing a hurting person needs to hear.

Will your story be the one that's passed down from generation to generation, influencing others?

It could be, if you're willing to share.

MARY, MOTHER OF JESUS: *Big Girls Do Cry*

❖

"Blessed are those who mourn, for they will be comforted."
MATTHEW 5:4 NIV

A grim parade marched through Jerusalem. Roman soldiers shoved spectators aside. Condemned prisoners, except for tortured, bloody Jesus, carried crosses to their execution. Crowds followed, including women who screamed and wept at His doom.

Did Mary, His mother, lead them? Or join them when she heard the horrible news? The Bible only tells us she stood near His cross with relatives and friends as Jesus writhed in pain. She may have cried more tears than she had in her entire life.

Jesus had told mourners, "Daughters of Jerusalem, do not weep for me; weep for yourselves and for your children" (Luke 23:28 NIV). At the cross, He again focused not on Himself, but on Mary's welfare. Jesus, the "man of sorrows" (Isaiah 53:3 KJV), had wept when His dear friend Lazarus died (John 11:35). He understood Mary's grief and did what He could to comfort her. Apparently Jesus' brothers, who earlier disowned Him, had disowned Mary, too. Despite His agony, Jesus ensured that John, the only one of the Twelve present, would take care of her.

Jesus' mother was not one of the first witnesses to His resurrection, that incredible demonstration of His power that consoles all who mourn. But Acts 1:14 states that Mary—and Jesus' brothers!—were present at Pentecost. There, she received ultimate assurance as the Comforter baptized them all.

RUTH: *The Truth about Beauty*

--- ❖ ---

"Now do as I tell you—take a bath and put on perfume and dress in your nicest clothes. Then go to the threshing floor, but don't let Boaz see you until he has finished eating and drinking."

RUTH 3:3 NLT

Naomi's advice to Ruth on the day of the harvest celebration reminds us of preparing for a prom. Take a bath and add a touch of perfume. Put on your best clothes and apply your makeup skillfully. The rest of Naomi's advice borders on scandalous: wait until Boaz is full, drunk, and ready to sleep. Sleep at his feet, showing your willingness to be his wife.

In recent years, the beauty pageant industry has captured public attention. By the time girls become teenagers, winning takes more than physical beauty. To win, a young lady must show poise, personality, talent, and intelligence.

Boaz had already seen Ruth's inner beauty. Her hard work and concern for Naomi first drew his attention. Her modest demeanor and care among strangers brought out his urge to protect her. Now came the time to take extra care with her appearance, to turn Boaz's head and convince him, once and for all, that he wanted her for his wife.

God frequently informs us that He looks at our hearts, not our appearance. But there are places, as here with Ruth and later with Esther, where a woman's beauty is celebrated. God made us beautiful, inside and out.

MAACHAH: *God's Good Plan*

And in Gibeon dwelt the father of Gibeon, Jehiel,
whose wife's name was Maachah.
1 CHRONICLES 9:35 KJV

Maachah is listed in the family tree of Saul, who was anointed king by the prophet Samuel. As she raised her children and grandchildren, Maachah had no idea that one of her grandsons would be anointed king in Israel.

Likewise, we don't know the plans God has for us. We don't know the role we will play in building His kingdom, but we can trust in God's good plan. As Jeremiah 29:11 (NIV) says, God has a fabulous future in mind for us. " 'I know the plans I have for you,' declares the LORD, 'plans to prosper you and not to harm you, plans to give you hope and a future.' "

Our responsibility is to trust God and to obey Him. Not doing so can bring God's good plans to a halt. Unfortunately, Maachah's grandson Saul was not king for long because he did not seek God.

When we think about the important tasks of our lives and futures, let's be sure to follow sound biblical advice, "Acknowledge the God of your father, and serve him with wholehearted devotion and with a willing mind, for the LORD searches every heart and understands every desire and every thought. If you seek him, he will be found by you" (1 Chronicles 28:9 NIV).

BERNICE: *Brick Wall*

— ❖ ❖ ❖ —

The next day Agrippa and Bernice came with great pomp and entered the audience room with the high-ranking military officers and the prominent men of the city. At the command of Festus, Paul was brought in. . . . So Paul motioned with his hand and began his defense.
ACTS 25:23; 26:1 NIV

Bernice, one of the Bible's bad girls, had an extensive sexual history. She was married three times; but between two of those marriages and after the last one, historians suspect she had an illicit relationship with her brother, Agrippa, whom she appears with here in Festus's audience room as the governor of Judea and her brother were trying to settle Paul's case.

Though she had nothing to do with deciding the case, Bernice heard Paul's defense against the accusations the Jewish leaders had made against him. That included his testimony of his conversion.

Though the apostle spoke to all three listeners, his testimony didn't halt Bernice's sin. If anything, her sexual exploits increased afterward. Sometimes no godly words impact a hardened heart.

Chances are good that at some time we will all meet women who have a similar history, and they may not respond to the good news we share. Yet just as Paul witnessed to Bernice, hit a brick wall, but didn't let that stop him from sharing the Gospel message, neither should we. We never know which seemingly hard heart will open at the hearing of God's Word.

HAGAR: *Pondering God's Questions*

—— ···◦◆◦··· ——

The angel said to her, "Hagar, Sarai's servant,
where have you come from, and where are you going?"
GENESIS 16:8 NLT

Hagar was lost and confused. She ran away from her
mistress, Sarah. She escaped into the desert. In the dryness of this
unknown land, God sent an angel not to reprimand for her for fleeing, but
to ask her questions.

Where have you come from?

Where are you going?

Through these two simple questions, God clarifies Hagar's next steps
in life. God didn't abandon her in her time of need. He came to Hagar,
giving her a new perspective through His straightforward guidance about
where her path led.

God comes to us, too, in times when we need discernment. If we feel
lost and confused, God lights our way with His presence and direction.

Right now is God asking us those same two questions?

Where have you come from? Reviewing our roots and routes we've
traveled in the past may reveal what we value and reassure us of God's past
and ongoing presence.

Where are you going? Spending time with God, we rediscover the
deep desires God planted within us, and we talk with Him about our hopes
and dreams.

God's questions are designed not to condemn us but to free us from
confusion, doubt, and fear. His love is near, and He's waiting for us to
pause and spend some time with Him, seeking direction in our lives and
pondering His questions.

TAMAR: *The Importance of Sanctuary*

····· ❧ ·····

Her brother Absalom saw her and asked, "Is it true that Amnon has
been with you? Well, my sister, keep quiet for now, since he's your
brother. Don't you worry about it." So Tamar lived as a desolate woman
in her brother Absalom's house.
2 Samuel 13:20 nlt

Tamar's story is the stuff of nightmares. Like her, many women carry inward scars made by overwhelming trauma, by unavoidable evil.

As a daughter of King David, Tamar lived a sheltered life. With royal guards and a dozen or so brothers, she had reason to feel safe. Instead, her brother Amnon attacked her. After he left, her knight in shining armor, her brother Absalom, arrived. He promised her justice. Sadly, unbelievably, David did nothing to intervene.

The fact that Tamar's attacker came from within her own family multiplied the shock and pain. We can only guess the emotions that stampeded through her. In addition to the sadness and loneliness that scriptures mention, she might have felt shame, anger, helplessness. In today's jargon, she probably suffered from PTSD, posttraumatic stress disorder.

Absalom provided the most important element for healing: sanctuary. In the quiet and solitude of his home, with servants to tend to her physical wounds, she began the road to recovery.

Sanctuary comes in many forms, from a new address to counselors and support groups.

Whatever direction we take, sanctuary is God's gift on the return to wholeness.

MIRIAM: *The Prophetess*

 ··· ✦ ✦ ···

*Let them praise his name with dancing and make music to him
with timbrel and harp. For the LORD takes delight in his people;
he crowns the humble with victory.*

PSALM 149:3–4 NIV

For decades, Miriam had watched her people, Israel,
endure the Egyptians' cruelty. Family and friends were at the mercy of
harsh taskmasters. As a young girl, Miriam kept silent about her baby
brother Moses, because one unguarded word could cause his death. When
their mother hid him among Nile River reeds, Miriam kept vigil and
watched God rescue Moses through Pharaoh's daughter.

Now elderly, Miriam watched as eighty-year-old Moses raised his staff
over the Red Sea at God's command. Trapped by Pharaoh's army, thousands
of Hebrews trembled as the ocean split before them. But they charged
forward. Miriam, too, walked on dry land, tons of water frothing on either
side of their path. They reached the opposite shore! When Egyptian
chariots attempted to follow, huge waves crashed down on them.

The people joined Miriam and Moses as they sang a victorious
doxology. Exodus 15:20–21 (NIV) calls her "Miriam the prophet" and tells
how she led her sisters in celebration: "Sing to the LORD, for he is highly
exalted. Both horse and driver he has hurled into the sea." Playing a
timbrel, Miriam shrugged off her age and danced with all her might. The
other women followed, stepping, twirling, singing for joy. Miriam, their
leader, had suffered with them. Now she would help guide them to the
Promised Land.

What song are we singing?

ADAH: *Split Allegiance?*

— ··· ❦ ··· —

Esau took his wives from the women of Canaan: Adah daughter of Elon the Hittite, and Oholibamah daughter of Anah and granddaughter of Zibeon the Hivite—also Basemath daughter of Ishmael and sister of Nebaioth.
GENESIS 36:2–3 NIV

Adah wasn't a Hebrew and probably didn't originally worship the Lord; she came from the Hittites, whose roots lay in modern-day Turkey. Obviously, some of her family had settled south of the Hittite empire, which only extended as far south as Damascus.

The Hittites worshipped a bewildering number of gods and easily added new, local deities to their pantheon. So it's likely that Adah would have had no problem adding Yahweh to her worship. But the idea of worshipping a single God would have been foreign to her. Since Esau didn't follow the earliest biblical pattern of cleaving to one wife and married only foreign women, he may not have had a deep relationship with God, and it may not have bothered him if his wives kept the idols of their families within their tents.

No matter what Adah's spiritual commitment was—or how little commitment she had—at some point she faced the temptation to worship wood or stone idols instead of the Lord.

It's a problem we still face today when temptations of the physical world seek to pull us far from God. Will we worship Him alone or seek to split our allegiance?

Division of the heart is also division of the soul.

What Did That Woman's Name Mean?

Just as today, some biblical names had meanings. Here are a few of those meanings, including names of some women in this book.

Sherah: Kindred

Shimeath: Annunciation

Shimrith: Female guard

Shiphrah: Brightness

Shomer: Keeper

Shua: A cry

Shuah: Dell

Susanna: Lily

LOT'S WIFE: *A Fatal Glance Backward*

— ··· ❖ ··· —

But Lot's wife looked back, and she became a pillar of salt.
GENESIS 19:26 NIV

Lot's wife lived with her family in the city of Sodom. The lifestyle of the Sodomites got so evil that God determined to completely destroy Sodom and the nearby city Gomorrah. However, in deference to Abraham's plea, God sent angels to evacuate Lot and his family before the destruction.

Lot's wife did not want to leave, and while she was eventually convinced to depart, she looked back. Her glance back was not one of curiosity, but of disobedient hesitation. She didn't want to leave the evil she had known in Sodom. As a consequence, she was punished along with the people of Sodom.

Often, God offers us opportunity to escape evil and follow Him, but taking the escape route means leaving a familiar lifestyle. Regret, fear of moving on, longing for comforts we once loved tempt us to look back. However, when God calls, we must embrace Him, His ways, and the journey He calls us to.

As Jesus told His followers, "Anyone who puts a hand to the plow and then looks back is not fit for the Kingdom of God" (Luke 9:62 NLT).

When we move forward with Jesus, we can be confident that we are following the One who knows the way to an abundant, satisfying life.

TAMAR: *The Dilemma*

— ···❖··· —

Judah recognized them and said, "She is more righteous than I, since I wouldn't give her to my son Shelah." And he did not sleep with her again.
GENESIS 38:26 NIV

Tamar was in a fix.

Years earlier, her father had arranged her marriage to Judah the Hebrew's oldest son. Er was a poor excuse for a man. He died young, leaving her childless. Following custom, she next married his younger brother, so that their first son would continue Er's name.

Her second husband refused to give her any children, and he died. Judah sent her to live with her parents until his youngest son reached marriageable age. Tamar lived in limbo for years. Judah's third son reached marriageable age, and his wife died. Either father or son could have performed the duty of giving her an heir, but they refused.

When she learned her father-in-law had business in town, she decided to take the matter into her own hands. Hiding her identity beneath a prostitute's veil, she offered herself at the side of the road. Judah slept with her. When she became pregnant, Judah acknowledged his mistake and gave her a place in his home.

God placed the bloodline for the Messiah on a slender thread: a woman who risked everything to give Judah an heir.

Like Judah and Tamar, we might find ourselves in situations that call for unconventional methods. When life hands us lemons, let's ask God for His recipe for lemonade.

HEPHZIBAH: *Prayers Eventually Answered*

—— ••• ❧❦❧ ••• ——

> *Manasseh was twelve years old when he became king, and he reigned in Jerusalem fifty-five years. His mother's name was Hephzibah.*
> 2 KINGS 21:1 NIV

Hephzibah is only mentioned briefly in the Bible. She gave birth to one of the worst kings of Judah. Manasseh, her son, promoted the worship of Baal and neglected the heritage of his roots. He was only twelve years old when he became king and ruled his territory for fifty-five years.

Hephzibah had married Hezekiah, a king who "did right in the eyes of the Lord." We can assume as parents they raised their son in the faith of their fathers. What happened?

We wonder if they fretted over their son's evil decisions. Did they have grand hopes and dreams for their son? Perhaps they prayed for him.

Hephzibah probably didn't live long enough to see the results of her prayers, but 2 Chronicles tells us that at the end of Manasseh's life he got rid of the false gods and restored Judah to the faith of his ancestors. In the end he came back to God.

Eventually her prayers were answered. God does respond to our requests, but often on a different time schedule than we would like. Our job is to be faithful. Our work is to hope and pray. We are called to look to God, who will come and restore His people to Himself once again.

Hephzibah persisted in prayer. Manasseh abandoned God, but God didn't desert him. Our call is to persist in prayer, too, knowing God will never abandon us.

PILATE'S WIFE: *Not-So-Sweet Dreams*

Does not wisdom call out? Does not understanding raise her voice? . . . "Listen, for I have trustworthy things to say; I open my lips to speak what is right."
PROVERBS 8:1, 6 NIV

"What a headache!" Pilate's wife, Claudia Procula, shoved silken quilts aside.

Echoes of her husband's voice and soldiers' feet from Antonia Fortress had not disturbed her sleep. As Roman governor of Judea, Pilate sometimes handled difficult situations this early.

It was the terrifying nightmare that still roiled inside her. Claudia shuddered. She could not remember details, but the dream involved the famous rabbi, Jesus. And Pilate.

A mob's roar swelled outside. Claudia choked on the drink her maid had brought. "What is happening?"

The maid said, "It's the Jewish religious leaders again."

Oh, no. Pilate's career had barely survived earlier confrontations with them. "What do they want this time?"

"They brought Jesus of Nazareth to be judged—"

"No!" Claudia screamed. "Call Marcus. Now!"

The trusted servant carried Claudia's message to Pilate: "Don't have anything to do with that innocent man, for I have suffered a great deal today in a dream because of him" (Matthew 27:19 NIV). Though Caesar Augustus's granddaughter, Claudia could not overrule her husband's decision, but she could tell him the truth.

Like Claudia, we find ourselves in situations over which we have no control. Will our efforts change circumstances? Hers did not, and we may never know if ours will. But we must tell the truth.

MARY, MOTHER OF JAMES AND JOSEPH:
Valued Disciple

Many women were there, watching from a distance. They had followed
Jesus from Galilee to care for his needs. Among them. . .[was] Mary
the mother of James and Joseph.
MATTHEW 27:55–56 NIV

Women, like Mary the mother of James and Joseph, played a
significant role in Jesus' ministry. Jesus, in contrast to many rabbis of His
time, valued women as disciples and friends. He spent time, discussed
important spiritual issues, and spoke of them with affection and respect.

Mary, the mother of James and Joseph, was one of the women who
heroically followed Jesus to attend to His needs. The Bible says she was
present as He hung on the cross and died.

We can only imagine the feelings and the conversations Mary and her
friends had as they watched Jesus die. That day their loyalty to their teacher
included pain and possibly some second-guessing as they wondered why
He was suffering rather than triumphing. But imagine the joy they felt when
a few days later they met their resurrected Savior and friend.

Often life includes suffering. We must remember that suffering is not
the end of the story. God has our lives in His hands, and He will work
good in our difficulties. Mary learned that firsthand and had grounds to
agree with Peter who said, "So then, those who suffer according to God's
will should commit themselves to their faithful Creator and continue to do
good" (1 Peter 4:19 NIV).

THE ANGRY WOMAN: *A Din in His Ears*

——— ••• ✥•✥ ••• ———

It's better to live alone in the desert than with a
quarrelsome, complaining wife.
PROVERBS 21:19 NLT

The poor fellow who married this woman may have known she would be a challenge, even before their wedding day, but he probably never expected to hear her voice din in his ears all day long, every day. Now he'd rather live all on his own, far from any human, because he's so tired of the noise.

Even if we're not married, we can relate. Angry people are never pleasant to be around, and we'd do almost anything to get away from them, especially when their voices rise. There's a reason why God discourages His people from getting caught up in anger, and we know it as soon as the screaming starts. Nothing kills any kind of relationship more quickly than a consistently angry response. Quarrels never add to understanding, and complaints never solve problems.

We all can experience life's imperfections, but anger shouldn't overpower us, or the resulting complaints and quarrels could ruin our opportunity for a happy life. On the other hand, those who consistently confess anger, give over hurts to God, and seek to live for Him in an uncomplaining way can find great blessing in the less-than-perfect life that they're seeking to bring ever more in line with His will.

ESTHER: *Every Life Is a Story*

— ❖ —

And the king loved Esther more than any of the other young women.
He was so delighted with her that he set the royal crown on her head
and declared her queen instead of Vashti.

ESTHER 2:17 NLT

Mystery, suspense, and uncertainty fill the pages in the book of Esther.

Around 479 BC, in Persia, an orphan, Esther, is raised by her cousin. One day, the king declares a nationwide beauty contest. Esther wins and becomes queen. But the new queen has a secret that could put her life in danger, if the king found out.

In the end her secret about her Jewish heritage becomes a tool God uses to save not only Esther, but all the Jewish people. What a moving tale of courage, guidance, and intrigue this book tells.

Every life is a story with times of uncertainty and mystery. In times of doubt we hesitate over which direction to take and seek the advice of others who are wiser than we. Often, as we look back upon our journey, we see God's providence. He has been with us all along, but only in retrospect do we clearly see His hand.

God in His grace walks with us in every word of our story. He stays with us amid points of fear and doubt. Like Esther, we gratefully find His strength, which enables us to meet the challenges along the way.

God has already written the conclusion of all believers' stories, and each has a victorious ending full of courage and jubilation.

TAPHATH: *Doing God's Business*

— ···◆◆◆··· —

Solomon had twelve district governors over all Israel, who supplied
provisions for the king and the royal household. Each one had to provide
supplies for one month in the year. . . . Ben-Abinadab—in Naphoth Dor
(he was married to Taphath daughter of Solomon).
1 KINGS 4:7, 11 NIV

The nation of Israel enjoyed its largest expanse during the
reigns of David and Solomon. Solomon amassed great riches and built
both the temple and the royal house. Such a large enterprise required a
large administration. The fourth chapter of 1 Kings starts by describing his
cabinet, everyone from the high priest to the man in charge of forced labor.

The chapter continues with governors, twelve in all, although they
didn't represent the twelve tribes per se. In addition to their administrative
duties, each governor was responsible for providing food for the royal
household for one month out of the year.

Two of Solomon's sons-in-law became governors. Ben-Abinadab was
married to Taphath. They governed a region located within the tribe of
Manasseh.

Taphath married an able administrator. We don't know how much she
had to do with his career, since women of that day were rarely involved in
business. But perhaps, as daughter of a king, she helped keep the wheels
of the kingdom running. Did she arrange special events and act as their
hostess? If so, her ministry echoed today's women who host church events,
cook for a crowd, run food pantries, and provide meals for the homebound.

Like Taphath, let us seek our place in God's "business" and work with
others for the good of all.

A Prudent Wife: *Unappreciated?*

·••· ❦·❦ ·••·

Houses and wealth are inherited from parents,
but a prudent wife is from the LORD.
PROVERBS 19:14 NIV

The Merriam-Webster Dictionary defines prudence as "(1) the ability to govern and discipline oneself by the use of reason, (2) sagacity or shrewdness in the management of affairs, (3) skill and good judgment in the use of resources, (4) caution or circumspection as to danger or risk."

Positive qualities? We probably would agree. Yet Top 40 love songs never mention prudence. Few bachelors and bachelorettes include it on their dream-mate lists.

King Solomon, the wisest man who ever lived, recognized that a wife who loves her family and uses good judgment and practical expertise contributes more than a rich inheritance. She is a special gift from God.

Solomon did not limit this insight to issues involving wives. He urged everyone to use prudence in handling daily affairs and dealing with other people. The king valued it as one of the bases for his book: "The proverbs of Solomon son of David, king of Israel: for gaining wisdom and instruction; for understanding words of insight; for receiving instruction in prudent behavior, doing what is right and just and fair" (Proverbs 1:1–3 NIV).

In today's reality-show, post-it-all-on-Facebook, Tweet-your-rage culture, Solomon's counsel still stands, a guide not only for wives and marriages, but for an entire society that would do well to relearn the meaning and merit of prudence.

HANNAH: *Surrendering All to the Lord*

— ••• ❖ ❖ ••• —

"I asked the LORD to give me this boy, and he has granted my request.
Now I am giving him to the LORD, and he will belong to the LORD his whole life."
And they worshiped the LORD there.
1 SAMUEL 1:27–28 NLT

Hannah desperately wanted a child. With a broken heart, she begged God to answer her prayer. Because she was praying so hard, the priest Eli thought she was drunk.

She poured out her anguish and pain-filled heart to God, lifting up her hands in submission to Him. Hannah let go and surrendered all.

In yielding even her deepest desire to God, giving everything to Him, she found peace and purpose. She found her heart overflowing with joy, no longer empty and barren. When she left the temple that day, she really didn't have the answer to her prayer, but she believed. She left clinging to her faith that her deep desire was in God's hands.

God can and will satisfy our deepest desires, too. He plants them inside of us, nurtures their discovery and growth, and waits for us to come to Him with open hands, asking for His blessing. When we surrender all to the Lord, life changes.

God welcomes us to take our troubles to him. Prayer is powerful when we relinquish the very thing we are requesting. When we give God even our highest dreams and our most desperate longings, He holds them tenderly for us. His love and presence satisfy our deepest wants and needs.

What Did That Woman's Name Mean?

Just as today, some biblical names had meanings. Here are a few of those meanings, including names of some women in this book.

Syntyche: Accident

Tabitha: The gazelle

Tamar: Palm tree

Taphath: Drop of ointment

Thamar: Palm tree

Timna: Restraint

Tirzah: Delightsomeness

Tryphena: Luxurious

Deborah the Nurse: *Positive Impact*

Soon after this, Rebekah's old nurse, Deborah, died. She was buried beneath the oak tree in the valley below Bethel. Ever since, the tree has been called Allon-bacuth (which means "oak of weeping").

GENESIS 35:8 NLT

Rebekah's nurse, Deborah, had been with her for a long time. As a child, Deborah would have cared for her. When Rebekah was grown, the family sent Deborah with the new bride to her distant home as Rebekah traveled to marry Isaac (Genesis 24:59). Deborah would have continued to fulfill her nursing role by tenderly helping Rebekah raise her boys, Esau and Jacob.

After the boys were grown and settled, Deborah died, and her master and mistress took care of her burial. Obviously, they did more than simply place her body in the ground, when you consider the name her burial place was given. Rebekah must have greatly loved her nurse and grieved her loss deeply. The two women had shared so many years and experiences.

To be important in our lives, people need not have impressive jobs or a lot of money. They need not be well known in our community. All they must do is have a positive impact on us. That can happen whether, like Deborah, they've been in our lives for years, or whether we've known them only a few days—it doesn't take long for a gentle hand or voice to win our hearts.

What gentle words or touches can help us win hearts today?

MAAKAH: *Queen Mother Deposed*

He even deposed his grandmother Maakah from her position as queen mother, because she had made a repulsive image for the worship of Asherah.
1 KINGS 15:13 NIV

Maakah, Absalom's daughter, had become the queen mother. Her grandson Asa had become king and, following his great-great-grandfather David's example, he implemented many reforms in response to God's commands. However, Maakah resisted this change for good.

Maakah longed to continue in worship with which she was familiar, and she made an image to celebrate the goddess Asherah, who was the consort of El. The image she made was an Asherah pole, which was probably a wooden likeness of the goddess. Maakah's creation of this abominable image was probably a deliberate attempt to counter the religious reforms her grandson was instituting. As a result, Asa deposed Maakah.

Change is always difficult. As much as we long to be fully God's, sometimes, like Maakah, we find ourselves in a position in which we resist change and cling to sinful ways that lead to destruction. We can ask God to help us fully embrace His ways, keeping in mind the admonition in Hebrews 12:1 (NLT), "Let us strip off every weight that slows us down, especially the sin that so easily trips us up. And let us run with endurance the race God has set before us."

THE WOMAN SUFFERING FROM BLEEDING: *Believe!*

* * *

*Just then a woman who had suffered for twelve years with constant bleeding
came up behind him. She touched the fringe of his robe, for she thought,
"If I can just touch his robe, I will be healed."*
MATTHEW 9:20–21 NLT

Making her way through the crowd of people, the woman
who had spent years suffering from bleeding sought healing from Jesus.
Her belief that Christ could make her life different propelled her through
the crowd and past her fears. Upon nearing Christ, she literally reached out
in faith and grabbed hold of Him. Her life was transformed.

When Jesus enters our life, it changes. And it continues to do so. God
tells us in Isaiah to not dwell on the way life used to be: "Forget the former
things; do not dwell on the past. See, I am doing a new thing! Now it
springs up; do you not perceive it?" (Isaiah 43:18–19 NIV).

Healed of her affliction, this woman could begin a new season in her
life. What did she do with this new beginning? Did she share what Jesus
had done for her? Did she find ways to support His ministry? Did she tell
others to not give up?

When we face tough times, do we believe God has something in mind
for us? Do we approach Jesus in faith? Do we reach out ready to grab hold of
Him? Trust, reach, and be transformed. It happened then, it happens now.

Believe it!

A Quarrelsome Wife:
Marriage Repair for Dummies

A quarrelsome wife is like the dripping of a leaky roof in a rainstorm.
PROVERBS 27:15 NIV

Sooner or later, a window-rattling gale exposes defects in a house. A home owner may find herself setting out buckets in the wee hours to catch rain dripping through the ceiling. If the leak is not repaired, the next storm will cause more damage. If neglect continues, the entire ceiling may crash down.

Just as a tempest reveals a leaky roof, trouble uncovers problems in a marriage. When inevitable financial, health, or relationship difficulties occur, a partner may drip-drip-drip frustration and criticism on her spouse. If the couple does not deal with it, further injury might destroy the protection a good marriage provides a husband, wife, and their children.

How much simpler to fix the initial problem. Better yet, Benjamin Franklin's "an ounce of prevention is worth a pound of cure" applies doubly to marriages and roofs! Prayerful marital maintenance, with encouragement and advice from experts, can help keep a relationship strong, even amid storms.

In another proverb, King Solomon says, "The wise woman builds her house, but with her own hands the foolish one tears hers down" (Proverbs 14:1 NIV).

No wife can maintain a strong marriage alone. But one who is proactive in building rather than weakening her marriage pleases God and encourages her husband to obey Him as well.

REBEKAH: *Move Forward with Confidence*

———— ••• ❧ ❧ ••• ————

So they called Rebekah and asked her, "Will you go with this man?"
"I will go," she said.
GENESIS 24:58 NIV

If ever a match was made in heaven, the marriage between Isaac and Rebekah was.

Abraham sent his faithful servant Eliezer to find Isaac a wife from the land of his fathers. He had only one stipulation: Isaac must not leave the land where God had led Abraham, decades before his birth.

After meeting Rebekah, Eliezer was convinced she was the one for Isaac. Excited, he proposed the arranged marriage. Her family agreed, but they asked Rebekah to wait. Perhaps they hoped Isaac would join her.

Sight unseen, Rebekah agreed to leave immediately. Her decision made the marriage binding and legal before they had a ceremony. We don't read "eccentric" into her willingness to leave with the unknown man. We call her romantic and courageous, a woman of faith.

When she spotted her husband for the first time, Rebekah jumped down from her camel, and he promptly took her to his mother's tent.

When faced with life-changing choices, Rebekah acted quickly and decisively. When God calls us to act, may we move forward with the same confidence.

ABIGAIL: *A King's Counselor*

—— ···❧·❦··· ——

*"When the Lord. . .has appointed him ruler over Israel, my lord will not
have on his conscience the staggering burden of needless bloodshed
or of having avenged himself. And when the Lord your God
has brought my lord success, remember your servant."*
1 SAMUEL 25:30–31 NIV

Abigail spoke these words to dissuade David from attacking
her land and killing her family and servants, simply because her husband,
Nabal, had foolishly and rudely refused to give him well-deserved aid. One
gentle reminder of how David's actions would look in the future deterred
the yet-uncrowned king of Israel from exacting bloody revenge against
Abigail's selfish spouse—and on everything he loved or owned.

Abigail had ridden to David with gifts of food and had humbly thrown
herself at the warrior-king's feet. Taking her husband's wrongs on herself,
she'd apologized before giving David this wise counsel not to follow his
first inclination. Perhaps her speech also made the king recognize all the
innocent people he'd be harming if he responded in anger; David quickly
backed out of his harsh retribution plan.

Abigail's humble reaction, so different from her husband's proud
refusal, saved her whole household and kept a king from sin. Recognizing
her wisdom and humility, David remembered her, after her husband's
death, and was moved to marry this remarkable woman.

People love to tell us, "No good deed goes unpunished." But that isn't
necessarily true in God's economy. Like Abigail, will we bravely do the
good thing, follow God's command, and gain His rewards?

HERODIAS'S DAUGHTER: *Fifteen Minutes of Fame*

On Herod's birthday the daughter of Herodias danced for the guests and pleased Herod so much that he promised with an oath to give her whatever she asked. Prompted by her mother, she said, "Give me here on a platter the head of John the Baptist."

MATTHEW 14:6–8 NIV

If you could have anything in the entire world, what would you request? Herodias's daughter, following her mother's orders, asked for John the Baptist's head on a platter.

The Bible tells us the rest of John's story but never again mentions Herodias's daughter. After her famous dance and gruesome request, we don't know how she felt, where she lived, or if she ever experienced any remorse. We don't know the end of her story.

We read about strange events in the news. People earn their "fifteen minutes of fame" for odd, stupid, or horrific exploits. Sometimes reporters follow up at certain anniversaries, following events, and explore what happened to a person at a later date in life.

What would the television camera capture of our own journey? What would they say about our lives in fifteen-minute glimpses? And ten years after the fact, where would we be? Still sinning? Still struggling? Or finally living a forgiven and transformed life?

We don't know what will happen in the future and how events of today will affect us, but God does. He knows how we feel. We can grow and learn from any of life's experiences, good or bad, and bring glory to God through our words and actions.

What will you do with your fifteen minutes?

RACHEL: *Was She for Real?*

---   ❖   ---

Let us purify ourselves from everything that contaminates body and spirit,
perfecting holiness out of reverence for God.
2 Corinthians 7:1 niv

Rachel appeared the perfect wife for Jacob. His parents, Isaac and Rebekah, fearful he would marry an idolatrous Canaanite, had sent to faraway relatives to find a spouse. Rachel was the drop-dead-gorgeous daughter of Laban, Rebekah's brother. Jacob fell in love with her immediately.

But Laban deceived Jacob into first marrying Leah, Rachel's sister. Sibling rivalry burgeoned (Genesis 29–30), as Jacob made his preference for Rachel obvious. When Leah produced sons—a cultural mandate for wives—and Rachel remained childless, the favored sister exploded with jealousy. Rachel blamed Jacob for her infertility. Having given her maid to him, she regarded the resulting sons as points she scored against Leah. Rachel did recognize that God gave her Joseph, though her son's name means "may he add."

Rachel's worst indictment, however, occurred when she stole her father's gods (Genesis 31:34). Did she spite Laban because of the marital messes he created? Or perhaps she could not bear to leave the idols behind.

Unlike Rachel, her son Joseph loved God without reservation. His faith helped his family—and both Egypt and Israel—survive.

God can use us, even when we, like Rachel, are less than perfect. But how much better to follow Him with all our hearts!

What Did That Woman's Name Mean?

Just as today, some biblical names had meanings. Here are a few of those meanings, including names of some women in this book.

Tryphosa: Luxuriating

Zebudah: Gainfulness

Zeruiah: Wounded

Zibiah: Gazelle

Zillah: Shade

Zilpah: Trickle

Zipporah: Bird

Zobebah: Canopy

ZERESH: *Poor Adviser*

His wife Zeresh and all his friends said to him. . .
ESTHER 5:14 NIV

Haman had a lot going for him: money, position, and the king's ear. He had a wife, Zeresh, and a group of friends. He would have been content had it not been for his hatred of Mordecai. Mordecai refused to bow down to Haman, and it drove Haman crazy. When Haman shared this with his wife and friends, they advised him to have Mordecai impaled on a tall pole.

A wife is supposed to be a helpmate, someone who will offer you sound advice. Did Zeresh think before suggesting Haman should impale Mordecai? Maybe she got caught up in the suggestions of Haman's friends and went along with what they advised. Perhaps she'd spent so much time around Haman that she picked up his bad habit of rash speaking. Whatever the reason, Zeresh's advice led to Haman's death.

Are we the type of people who give advice based on what we think the other person wants to hear, instead of what he or she needs to hear? If Zeresh had pointed out the pluses in Haman's life or advised him to think through what he was about to do, things might have turned out differently. Instead, Zeresh paid for her bad counsel by losing her husband and, later on, her sons.

Let's speak with wisdom and courage. We and the people we're advising will be glad we did.

PETER'S MOTHER-IN-LAW:
Served by the Perfect Guest

---·· ❖ ·❖· ❖ ··---

Simon's mother-in-law was in bed with a fever, and they immediately told
Jesus about her. So he went to her, took her hand and helped her up.
The fever left her and she began to wait on them.
MARK 1:30–31 NIV

When a high fever stole the energy Peter's mother-in-law
usually displayed, she finally went to bed. Her daughter said that Jesus and
His disciples were nearing Capernaum. Peter and his brother, Andrew,
spent more and more time with Jesus. Could He really be the Messiah they
all longed for?

No doubt Jesus and His entourage would stay awhile. So much to do—
the house to clean, linens to wash, bread to bake. Peter's mother-in-law
wanted to make Jesus welcome. Instead, she could hardly move, let alone
make preparations. Forced to hand the burden to her daughter, she hated
feeling helpless. Would she ever be well again?

A roughened but gentle hand took hers, awakening her from a stupor.
She cringed to see Jesus kneeling by her bed. What a sight she must have
been—matted hair, bloodshot eyes, sunken cheeks!

A cool current flowed through her with a mountain stream's freshness.
The desertlike fever vanished. Jesus' strong hand raised her to a sitting
position, then to her feet. Feeling like a new woman, she thanked Him
again and again for healing her.

But she soon hurried to the cooking fires, determined to make the best
dinner He had ever tasted.

What would we do for the One who heals us?

BILHAH: *Ungodly Choices*

❖

So Rachel gave her servant, Bilhah, to Jacob as a wife, and he slept with her. Bilhah became pregnant and presented him with a son. Rachel named him Dan, for she said, "God has vindicated me! He has heard my request and given me a son."

GENESIS 30:4–6 NLT

Polygamy was certainly not the Lord's design for marriage. Though it established the twelve tribes of Israel, God had still created one woman out of one man and designed them to be one flesh (Genesis 2:21–24).

Jacob's household became extremely complex after he agreed to marry two sisters. The women's resulting childbearing competition disrupted any sense of happiness Jacob and the woman he really loved, Rachel, might have had in family life. As if two wives weren't bad enough, barren Rachel increased the family's emotional pressure by having her servant, Bilhah, bear children for her. Sadly, powerless Bilhah had no control over her marriage, the two children she bore, or the rest of her life. Then after Rachel's death, Jacob's son Reuben slept with Bilhah, making things even more tense.

Though God brought good things out of awful situations, how much happier life might have been, especially for Bilhah, had this family followed His plan for marriage. But Jacob's family couldn't go back and eradicate those ungodly decisions that brought them to such a painful place.

If we seem stuck in a bad place, let's remember Bilhah and her family and follow God's plan, not some questionable plan of our own.

RUTH: *Loving the Unlovable*

- ··· ❧ ❧ ···

"The LORD has afflicted me; the Almighty has brought misfortune upon me."
So Naomi returned from Moab accompanied by Ruth the Moabite,
her daughter-in-law.
RUTH 1:21–22 NIV

Few words in scripture are as well known as Ruth's plea to her mother-in-law: "Intreat me not to leave thee. . .for whither thou goest, I will go; and where thou lodgest, I will lodge: thy people shall be my people, and thy God my God" (Ruth 1:16 KJV). Her words are held up as a pattern for husbands and wives.

Ruth spoke the words not to her husband, but to her mother-in-law, Naomi. They had grown close over the years, but the deaths of her husband and sons had turned Naomi into a bitter woman. When they returned to Bethlehem, Naomi's hometown, she gave voice to her bitterness. She doesn't sound very lovable.

Ruth had been at Naomi's side through the same depressing turns their lives had taken. As Naomi repeated her stories, Ruth was forced to relive her own losses. No one would have blamed Ruth if she had fled Naomi's company. How could one reproach her if she had complained?

Instead, Ruth loved Naomi, and it's shown by her actions. She traveled with her, provided for their needs, and heeded her advice. By the time Ruth handed her son to Naomi, her mother-in-law had changed.

If God puts us in close quarters with unpleasant people, let us love them by listening, respecting, and taking care of their needs. Leave it to God to heal their pain—through us.

ESTHER: *A Time for Courage and Wisdom*

— ⋯ ❧ ❧ ⋯ —

Mordecai sent this reply to Esther: "Don't think for a moment that because you're in the palace you will escape when all other Jews are killed. If you keep quiet at a time like this, deliverance and relief for the Jews will arise from some other place, but you and your relatives will die. Who knows if perhaps you were made queen for just such a time as this?"

ESTHER 4:13–14 NLT

"*For just such a time* as this" are the words that motivated Esther to act. She was the one. The only one who had the power, the position, and the possibility to save her people. Did she have the courage?

Crossroads similar to what Esther faced confront us, too. Should we speak up when we see injustice? What action should or could we take? Do we tell our coworkers and friends we don't like the gossip or making fun of others? How do we tackle the challenges that come with standing against routine tolerance of prejudices and inequality?

Life isn't always fair, but God is just. Turning to Him, we find the courage to act. Reading His Word and listening in prayer, we find the wisdom to know which direction to take. He will guide us on what battles to fight.

God needs willing warriors to defend the powerless and to help the poor. He will provide the time, the strength, and the courage—we just need to be open to His call for action. Perhaps right now we are the ones "for just such a time as this."

WIFE OF SEVEN BROTHERS: *No Cloudy Thinking*

··· ❦ ···

"Now then, at the resurrection, whose wife will she be of the seven,
since all of them were married to her?"
MATTHEW 22:28 NIV

The Sadducees were always interested in tripping Jesus up. They thought they had an opportunity to do this by using the example of this woman who had seven husbands. They had the law part correct. Moses had instructed that, if a man died without having children, his brother had to marry the widow and raise up offspring for him. After that, though, the Sadducees' understanding of the scripture failed.

Jesus responded that marriage will not look the same in heaven as it does here on earth. How shocked those listening must have been at His statement. Perhaps we're shocked, too. It's hard not comparing the familiar to the unfamiliar. To not take what we see and know and apply it to everything, including heaven.

Jesus goes on to further show them, and us, how cloudy our thinking can get: "You are in error because you do not know the Scriptures or the power of God" (Matthew 22:29 NIV). We, too, often fall into the trap of making God smaller and less powerful than He is. Doing this can create gaps in our faith and make us question God's capability.

The Sadducees viewed life through knowledge, not faith. We need to do the exact opposite and view life through faith. When we do, knowledge will come.

SAMSON'S WIFE: *Impossible Choice*

— ⋯ ⟡ ⋯ —

On the fourth day, they said to Samson's wife, "Coax your husband into explaining the riddle for us, or we will burn you and your father's household to death. Did you invite us here to steal our property?"
JUDGES 14:15 NIV

We don't even know her name.

Before Samson met Delilah, he fell in love with another Philistine woman. At the time, Israel was under the control of Philistia. They could grab anything they wanted from the Israelites. But Samson's love ran deep. The fathers arranged the marriage and the wedding proceeded.

His wife didn't return his feelings. She cried for all seven days of the wedding feast. When the guests asked her to learn the answer to Samson's riddle, she didn't hesitate. When they won the bet, Samson retaliated by killing thirty Philistines. He returned home without his wife.

The wedding guests had ensured her cooperation by threatening to burn her family to death. After Samson left, her father gave her to a member of the wedding party as a consolation prize. When Samson attacked again, the threats were carried out—death by fire.

Like other women past and present, Samson's wife appears as a pawn in the events circling her. All her choices felt equally dangerous. At what point could—should—this nameless woman have taken a stand?

We also may be faced with impossible choices. But God will give us the wisdom and courage to act.

ORPAH: *Do What Comes Naturally?*

⸻ ··· ❖◦❖ ··· ⸻

But those who turn to crooked ways, the LORD will banish with the evildoers.
PSALM 125:5 NIV

Orpah married Kilion (or Chilion), whose Hebrew family had moved to her native Moab. After Kilion died, Orpah, along with Ruth, her widowed sister-in-law, vowed to return with their mother-in-law, Naomi, to Israel to begin a new life. Maybe Naomi's kindness over the years influenced Orpah to consider leaving her own family. Perhaps Orpah had grown to appreciate Naomi's God.

But Naomi, grieving her dead husband and sons, painted a dismal picture of the young widows' future with her.

Orpah kissed her mother-in-law good-bye. As her well-being depended on marriage, Orpah's choice made sense. Her country and Israel had clashed for centuries; most Jewish men, unlike Kilion, would hesitate to wed an enemy. A man who shared Orpah's background presented a far better marriage prospect. Besides, though Orpah admired Naomi and her God, Yahweh seemed stricter than Moab's Chemosh and his female counterpart Astarte, the goddess of fertility. Did Orpah really want to spend a lifetime keeping all those commandments? She returned to her own people and her gods.

The Old Testament does not mention Orpah again, but rabbinical literature connects her with promiscuity resulting in pagan offspring who fought God's people—a marked contrast to Ruth's descendants, who include King David and Jesus Christ.

All because Orpah did what came naturally.

WISE WOMAN'S BUILDING PLAN: *A Solid Home*

The wise woman builds her house, but with her own hands
the foolish one tears hers down.
PROVERBS 14:1 NIV

A lot goes into constructing a home. Besides the building materials, there's an investment of time, energy, and money. You also need a supply of patience. Once the house is finished, there are other decisions to be made, such as decorating and landscaping.

Just as we choose what pictures to hang on the walls and what furniture to buy, we decide on the tone of our homes. Has each of us prepared a home where the tone is one of calmness and peace? Is God's Word taught in our homes? Do people leave our houses feeling encouraged after spending time there?

Or have we set a tone of discord, creating an atmosphere of agitation where our families feel uptight and no one feels welcome? The tone we set either keeps the walls sturdy or causes them to crack and eventually crash down around us.

Examine your home. Are you filling it with love, instruction, peace, forgiveness, compassion, and friendliness? Are you determined to not allow anything in your home that isn't beneficial to those living there?

If you find the tone of your home is better suited to demolition than building, take heart. With God's help it's not too late to make a change. A rebuilt, godly home will not always be stress-free, but if it's built upon the firm foundation of Christ, you can be assured it will stand.

AHINOAM: *Enjoy Today*

——— ···⚜··· ———

*David's two wives were Ahinoam from Jezreel and Abigail, the widow of
Nabal from Carmel. So David and his wives and his men and their families
all moved to Judah, and they settled in the villages near Hebron.*
2 SAMUEL 2:2–3 NLT

Before he was made king of Judah, David brought his family
and his following to Hebron, an important city of the Judean hill country.
They stayed there seven years before David captured Jerusalem and moved
his capital there. But those early years of his marriage to Ahinoam were not
peaceful. David's war continued as he battled Saul's son Ishbosheth for
Israel's throne.

Yet throughout the years that followed, did Ahinoam look back on
those years in the city where her son Amnon was born as the best of her
life? Though Jerusalem was grander than Hebron, her life there also held
awful troubles she could never have foreseen. In Jerusalem her son would
listen to bad advice and rape his half sister, Tamar, an action that began the
downward spiral of David's family life. And eventually Ahinoam's only son
would be killed by his angry half brother Absalom.

So often we look to the future, expecting better things. But God gives
us each day to enjoy. Are we delighting in today or only hoping for future
times? If so, let's keep in mind that those unknown days could end up
bringing more challenges than sunny moments. Let's make the most of each
one of the days God gifts us with.

JAIRUS'S DAUGHTER: *Taking Jesus' Hand*

❖

When Jesus arrived at the official's home, he saw the noisy crowd and heard the funeral music. "Get out!" he told them. "The girl isn't dead; she's only asleep." But the crowd laughed at him. After the crowd was put outside, however, Jesus went in and took the girl by the hand, and she stood up!

MATTHEW 9:23–25 NLT

Jairus's daughter was dead, and Jesus arrived too late to save her. When Jesus told the crowd she was only sleeping, everyone laughed at Him. They didn't believe Him. They knew what they had seen—the girl was dead. No hope. No other option. The end was final. The funeral music played.

But Jesus changed everything; His presence opened another possibility. With one touch He altered destiny, and His compassion created a new alternative ending. As He took her hand, she rose.

Jesus reaches out to us, too. When circumstances in our lives look grim and our choices are limited, God is there. When the only route ahead of us is dark and terrifying, He stays with us.

The God of hope is ever present. He creates options and shows us the next step. Others may laugh at our faith. They may not believe in what we know to be true. But we know the One whose touch heals and instills the courage to rise again.

God's love turns the funeral music into celebration of new life. New beginnings, fresh options, and renewed hope transform our expectations for the future.

Take Jesus' hand and rise up to enter God's new day.

WOMEN WHO FOLLOWED JESUS: *Faith in Action*

—— ···❧◦❧··· ——

Many women were there, watching from a distance. They had followed Jesus from Galilee to care for his needs.
MATTHEW 27:55 NIV

Jesus' death was witnessed by many, including Mary Magdalene, James and Joseph's mother, and the mother of Zebedee's sons.

How awful it must have been for these women to witness all that Jesus was going through. This wasn't just some person they had heard about. They had followed Jesus and were personally affected by His ministry. Now they were watching Him die a horrendous death on a cross.

In the Gospel of Luke, Jesus tells those around Him, "If any of you wants to be my follower, you must turn from your selfish ways, take up your cross daily, and follow me" (Luke 9:23 NLT). These women were living out this passage of scripture. They turned away from their fears, put aside their comfort, and risked possible persecution, because they desired to follow Jesus.

Not every place Jesus leads us is going to be comfortable. Our hearts will break now and then. We'll cry at injustice, fear the crowd pressing in around us, and wonder how people can treat Christ with such disdain. Yes, following Jesus can be challenging.

Yet these women show us it can be done. They remained faithful even though walking away would have been easier than watching Christ suffer and die. Their steadfastness is an example to us of what faith in action looks like.

Indexes

Scripture Index

Name Index

Author Index

Award-winning author and speaker *Darlene Franklin* recently returned to cowboy country—Oklahoma.

Faith Tibbetts McDonald is a writer and writing instructor who lives in State College, Pennsylvania, with her husband, Steve. With God's help, they are navigating the challenges of parenting three young adult children: Matthew, Phillip, and Carolyn. When she's not grading papers, Faith likes to read, write, and bike.

Pamela L. McQuade is a freelance writer and editor with dozens of projects to her credit. She has also coauthored *The Top 100 Men of the Bible* with her husband, Drew, under the name Drew Josephs.

Rachael Phillips is a freelance writer in Indiana. She is married with three children.

Martha Willey is married with three boys and works as a para-professional. Martha has contributed to numerous books published by Barbour, including the recently published *Every Good and Perfect Gift*.

Jean Wise is a writer, speaker, and retreat leader whose goal is "to know God and make Him known." She lives in northwest Ohio.